Saratoga and Yorktown: The History of the American Revolution's Most Important Campaigns

By Charles River Editors

Surrender of Burgoyne by John Trumbull

Introduction

Surrender of Lord Cornwallis by John Trumbull

The American Revolution is replete with seminal moments that every American learns in school, from the "shot heard 'round the world" to the Declaration of Independence, but the events that led up to the fighting at Lexington & Concord were borne out of 10 years of division between the British and their American colonies over everything from colonial representation in governments to taxation, the nature of searches, and the quartering of British regulars in private houses. From 1764-1775, a chain of events that included lightning rods like the Townshend Acts led to bloodshed in the form of the Boston Massacre, while the Boston Tea Party became a symbol of nonviolent protest.

The political and military nature of the Revolutionary War was just as full of intrigue. While disorganized militias fought the Battles of Lexington & Concord, George Washington would lead the Continental Army in the field while men like Thomas Jefferson drafted the Declaration of Independence in Philadelphia and Benjamin Franklin negotiated overseas in France. French forces would play a crucial role at the end of the war, and the Treaty of Paris would conclude the Revolution with one last great surprise.

At the end of 1776, the American war effort was on the verge of collapse, and despite Washington's success at Trenton, the British were confident that they could quell the rebellion in 1777. That winter, the British planned a complicated campaign in which British armies from Canada and New York would strike out across New England and link up, with the goal of cutting off the Northern colonies. Indeed, 1777 did prove to be the pivotal year of the war, but not in the way the British intended.

The British planned a three-pronged sweep through the northern colonies that would eventually end with the linking of three different forces. The design of the plan called for the capture of Philadelphia, as well as the colony of New York, and it aimed all but slice the rebellious colonies in two. The main thrust of the campaign was John Burgoyne's army of nearly 8,000 men, which started out from Quebec and began making its way south through New York. From the beginning, however, Burgoyne was not on the same page as William Howe. Burgoyne had concocted the campaign strategy and received approval from an intermediary, but Howe had informed that same intermediary that he could not meet up with Burgoyne in New York because he calculated he would be busy late into the year taking Philadelphia. It's unclear whether Burgoyne was ever informed of Howe's response, but unbeknownst to each other, the two commanders were not on the same page.

By July, Burgoyne had taken Fort Ticonderoga in New York, but as he tried to get a bearing on the coordinated strategy, the Americans shot another hole into the grand campaign at Fort Stanwix. The British and their Native American allies had inflicted some serious damage on militiamen near Fort Stanwix, but Arnold led an 800-man contingent to the outskirts of the fort and began to lay siege. Realizing that he would not win an open battle, Arnold resorted to subterfuge and succeeded into fooling the British allied Native Americans that he had a much larger force. When the British were left without their allies, Lieutenant Colonel Barry St. Leger decided to head back toward Quebec. His men would never link up with Burgoyne's as planned.

At the end of August, Burgoyne learned that St. Leger would not be linking up with him, and that he could not expect help from Howe near New York City or Philadelphia. Nevertheless, while worried about where he would camp his army for the winter, Burgoyne decided to keep advancing in September. Thus, instead of heading back to Ticonderoga, Burgoyne made Albany his target for winter camping, and he ordered his army forward until they were just a few miles north of Saratoga by mid-September.

Opposing the British were nearly 10,000 Americans led by General Horatio Gates, who had taken over for Philip Schuyler. With the advice of renowned Polish engineer, Thaddeus Kosciusko, Gates anchored his army's line from the Hudson River to bluffs known as Bemis Heights. Gates assumed direct command of the army's right wing, and he put Arnold in command of the left wing, which was stationed on Bemis Heights. Though the two had gotten along earlier in the war and Gates had been one of Arnold's strongest allies, he was apparently rubbed the wrong way when Arnold chose Schuyler allies for his staff. Gates despised Schuyler, and this led to animosity between Gates and Arnold as well due to both generals' obstinate personalities.

During the First Battle of Saratoga, fought on September 19, Burgoyne's army moved to flank

Arnold, who had anticipated an attack on his wing and had asked Gates to allow him to position his troops on Freeman's Farm to block a potential flank attack. Gates, however, anticipated a frontal assault and thus only allowed Arnold to send a small contingent of Daniel Morgan's riflemen and other light infantry to reconnoiter in that vicinity. As it turned out, that reconnaissance came into contact with Burgoyne's flank, starting the Battle of Freeman's Farm. Although the British won a tactical victory, the Americans inflicted nearly 600 casualties, about 10% of Burgoyne's effective fighting force.

Understandably, Arnold was miffed that the result took place because his advice had been ignored, and it boiled over into an all-out feud with Gates, who conspicuously refused to mention Arnold at all in the official account of the battle. At the same time, Gates removed Morgan's company from Arnold's command, bringing about a vocal shouting match between Gates and Arnold that resulted in Gates sidelining Arnold and telling him he was being replaced in command of that wing.

After the argument, Arnold began preparing to formally request a transfer to George Washington's command, while Gates continued to humiliate Arnold at the camp. It's still unclear why Arnold continued to stay with Gates' army, but it proved to be one of the most fortuitous decisions of the American Revolution.

Unbeknownst to the Americans at the time, Burgoyne was in contact with British General Sir Henry Clinton over whether Clinton could move diversionary forces in time to assist Burgoyne. Burgoyne went so far as to explain to Clinton that he would be forced to retreat by early October without reinforcements. As fate would have it, Clinton would actually begin moving forces that way and take some forts in the vicinity in early October, but his messengers announcing that to Burgoyne were captured. Burgoyne wouldn't learn about Clinton's movements until after the Battle of Bemis Heights.

In early October, the demoted Arnold got into one more argument with Gates after proposing an advance against the British. By this time, Gates had taken command of the left wing and promptly informed Arnold, "You have no business here." At the same time, when General Lincoln proposed similar advice, Gates took it and followed it. With a plan to attack both British flanks, the Battle of Bemis Heights started with the American advance on the left coming into contact with the British. The Americans began making progress on both sides of the British line, and British General Simon Fraser was mortally wounded on their right flank, helping the American cause.

As gunfire could be heard back at camp, Arnold only got more agitated at his situation. Unable to stand being sidelined any more, Arnold took off toward the right, where Enoch Poor's column was attempting to flank the British left. With this obvious defiance of orders and complete insubordination, Gates sent an aide after Arnold to bring him back to camp.

Thankfully, that aide, Major Armstrong, was unable to do so. To every soldier's surprise, General Arnold was soon spotted at the front leading the attack on a British redoubt. Arnold was so worked up that some believed he had been drinking. The British had been able to hold the redoubt with such spirit that Burgoyne wrote after the battle, "A more determined perseverance than they showed... is not in any officer's experience." However, it would be Arnold who persevered, and he led another charge through a gap between two British redoubts, allowing American troops to threaten the rear of British General Breymann's men in the redoubt. Showing absolutely no concern for his well-being, Arnold rode his horse up and down the line between the Americans and British.

During the attack, Breymann was killed and the Americans captured the redoubt. But near the end of the fighting, one of the final volleys hit Arnold in his leg and his horse, who fell onto the same leg and broke it. At that point, Arnold was finally brought back on a litter by Major Armstrong to camp.

By the time the decisive American victory was finished, Burgoyne had lost nearly 20% of his effective fighting during the battles at Saratoga, and after a few days his trapped army surrendered to the Americans.

In December 1776, Benjamin Franklin was sent by Congress to France to attempt to secure a critically needed alliance. Franklin was an ideal choice for Enlightened France, which revered Franklin for his scientific accomplishments and his known reputation as a brilliant man. Franklin had also been a diplomat before the Revolution, spending several years in London on behalf of the colonies. However, the French refused to provide more than arms and money throughout 1777, until they learned in December 1777 about Saratoga and Burgoyne's surrender. With that news, French King Louis XVI entered into a formal military alliance with the United States, and in February 1778, France joined the war.

Naturally, the accolades for Saratoga went to Gates as commanding general, while the grievously wounded Arnold would be recommissioned Major General Arnold with his proper relative rank restored. Even still, Gates failed to credit Arnold for the success at Saratoga, and his actions also came at an incredible cost: his leg was so shattered that doctors wanted to amputate it, failing to do so only at the threat of physical violence by Arnold himself. By setting the leg, it would remain two inches shorter than Arnold's other leg for the rest of his life. Arnold would be out of service for nearly half a year, and he would never truly be physically fit again. In that way, the very battle that may have won the Revolution also set in process a chain of events that led to the most notorious act of betrayal in American history.

Yorktown was a former tobacco trading post now in decline, not much bigger than a large village. But Yorktown was tucked away on the northern edge of the York peninsula in rural Virginia, and in 1781 it became the site of a brief siege between two small armies, fought with all the decorum and formality of 18th century European warfare. About 5,000 British and

Germans faced perhaps 18,000 Americans and French. After only three weeks the smaller garrison surrendered, tired and low on ammunition. Casualties for both sides totaled less than 1,000 dead and wounded.

By contrast, at the siege of Stalingrad 161 years later, 107,000 Germans surrendered to 1.2 million Russians after five months of desperate fighting. At least a million died. At Waterloo in 1815, 190,000 troops slugged it out, leaving 14,000 dead in 10 hours. Another siege would take place at Yorktown during the Civil War 81 years after the more famous siege. Yorktown does not rank as a major military engagement by the conventional criteria of size, duration or casualties, but this small scale encounter was one of the most decisive battles in military history. The fact that it was the last major battle of the American Revolution has ensured that every Briton and American has heard of it.

Yorktown's importance has led to a legacy full of legends, but as a campaign and siege, the history of the fighting at Yorktown is a fascinating story. Trapped at Yorktown by a combination of brilliant Allied generalship and a measure of bad luck, the British might still have hoped for rescue. They faced a mixed force, many of whom were ill-trained and ill equipped militia, while the British Army was then regarded as the most tactically proficient in the world. Lord Charles Cornwallis, their commander, had beaten a much larger American force that same spring, with his crack redcoats striding through the woods to eject Nathaniel Greene's well-positioned army from Guildford Courthouse. As he made his dispositions at Yorktown in September 1781, he had every reason to expect another British success. The ensuing siege panned out rather differently. On October 19, 1781, for just the second time during the war (the other at Saratoga), an entire British field army surrendered to the rebel patriots.

Planning the Saratoga Campaign

George Washington is perhaps the most famous American in history and is viewed as his country's greatest Revolutionary hero, but he and his Continental Army had a terrible year after the British evacuated Boston in March 1776. After the siege of Boston, Washington suspected that the British evacuated by sea to New York City, the next logical target in an attempt to end a colonial resurrection. He thus rushed his army south to defend the city.

Washington guessed correctly, but it would be to no avail. Unlike Boston, New York City's terrain featured few defensible positions. The city lacked a high point from which to launch a siege on an occupation, as the peninsula of Boston was fortunate to have. Moreover, Washington wasn't sure defending the city was necessary, hoping that an expedition launched toward Quebec like the one Benedict Arnold had led in late 1775 would keep the British away from New York. But Congress thought otherwise and demanded that Washington defend New York.

Washington thus did what he was told, to his demise. In the summer of 1776, the British conducted the largest amphibious expedition in North America's history at the time, landing over 20,000 troops on Long Island. British General William Howe, who had led the British at Bunker Hill and would later become commander in chief of the armies in North America, easily captured Staten Island, which Washington was incapable of defending without a proper navy. Washington's army attempted to fight, but Washington was badly outmaneuvered, and his army was nearly cut off from escape, and his withdrawal across New York City was enormously disorderly, with many of Washington's troops so scared that they deserted. Others were sick, with dysentery and smallpox plaguing the Continental Army in New York. In what was arguably the worst defeat of the Revolution, Washington was ashamed. He also felt betrayed, by both his troops and Congress.

To escape from New York, Washington led a tactical retreat across the East River and off Long Island in the middle of the night without British knowledge. This retreat prevented the annihilation of the colonial army in New York, but with Washington being pushed west across New Jersey and into Pennsylvania, Congress was forced to flee Philadelphia. And with this string of crucial British successes in 1776, the Revolution was on the brink of failure. The Continental Army, now in Pennsylvania, had lost over 5,000 men during its retreat through New York and New Jersey and now had fewer than 5,000 able soldiers. That winter, one of the men in camp, Thomas Paine, would write *The American Crisis*, beginning with the famous words, "These are the times that try men's souls."

After failing to bag Washington's army in New York, the British gave chase, but with the winter beginning, the British camped out on the New Jersey side of the Delaware River. In the 18th century, armies generally suspended their ongoing military campaigns during winter, allowing the colonists to plan ways to halt British momentum during the fighting months. A perfect example of that was Benedict Arnold's campaign to Quebec in 1775, which was a tactical defeat that succeeded in keeping the British in Canada from conducting a campaign until the spring of 1776.

With a beaten down army, American morale was low. Throughout all the colonies, many expressed doubts about the viability of the war. Washington knew he needed a big victory, after having spent the past six months suffering one defeat after the other. On the other hand, it seemed perfectly logical to camp out in Pennsylvania and wait until spring to resume fighting. But Washington's insistence on a big move was so resolute that he authorized an unorthodox decision on Christmas of 1776.

On Christmas night, Washington led his troops across the frigid and partially frozen Delaware River. Once on the other side, they advanced south to Trenton, where they attacked, captured and killed Hessian soldiers stationed there. The Hessians had celebrated Christmas and were completely unprepared for an attack. Only a handful of Americans were killed, while the Continental Army captured over 1,000 Hessian forces, and killed nearly 100.

Leutz's famous painting of Washington crossing the Delaware

The Battle of Trenton was indeed the decisive move Washington had hoped it would be. The British general, Lord Cornwallis, marched south from New York City through New Jersey to capture Trenton. Washington, however, moved to Cornwallis' rear and attacked the British at Princeton, New Jersey in January 1777, forcing the British to retreat to New York City for the rest of the winter.

Despite the victory, however, Washington faced an unprecedented crisis. Apart from the men recruited in Massachusetts before the creation of the Second Continental Congress, Washington's Army's 1-year recruitment term was now up. With the end of the year 1776, much of Washington's Army intended to finish. Washington had to urge Congress to make an important decision and extend enlistment terms. Fearing the creation of a permanent Army, many in Congress feared making this decision. In the end, however, they approved enlistment terms of three years or "until the war is finished." Crisis had been narrowly averted.

The campaign plan that brought about the Battle of Saratoga came from the pen of Major General John Burgoyne. Burgoyne had returned to England in November 1776 after having spent his summer helping to expel the American forces under Benedict Arnold from the St. Lawrence Valley. In London, aside from spending a good amount of time at the gaming tables, Burgoyne composed "Thoughts for Conducting the War from the Side of Canada," which proposed a change in British strategy. Rather than focusing on the New England region, Burgoyne proposed an invasion of New York from Canada, with a British force of about 7,000 strong moving south in a thrust. It aimed to capture Fort Ticonderoga, which Arnold had helped capture from the British in 1775, and from there the British would move toward Albany. Meanwhile, British troops under General Sir William Howe would move from New York City to Albany, and together, they would isolate New England. According to the plan, when the Americans under Washington moved from New Jersey to try to aid New England, Howe would crush the Continental Army and end the rebellion once and for all.

In conclusion, Burgoyne wrote, "Should it appear, upon examination of the really effective numbers of the Canada army, that the force is not sufficient for proceeding upon the above ideas with a fair prospect of success, the alternative remains of embarking the army at Quebec, in order to effect a junction with General Howe by sea, or to be employed separately to co-operate with the main designs, by such means as should be within their strength upon other parts of the continent. And though the army, upon examination of the numbers from the returns here, and the reinforcements designed, should appear adequate, it is humbly submitted, as a security against the possibility of its remaining inactive, whether it might not be expedient to entrust the latitude of embarking the army by sea to the commander in chief, provided any accidents during the winter, and unknown here, should have diminished the numbers considerably, or that the enemy, from any winter success to the southward, should have been able to draw such forces towards the frontiers of Canada, and take up their ground with such precaution, as to render the intended measure impracticable or too hazardous. But in that case it must be considered that more force would be required to be left behind for the security of Canada, than is supposed to be necessary when an army is beyond the lakes; and I do not conceive any expedition from the sea can be so formidable to the enemy, or so effectual to close the war, as an invasion from Canada by Ticonderoga. This last measure ought not to be thought of, but upon positive conviction of its necessity."

Burgoyne

An engraving of Arnold

An engraving of Howe

It helped that Burgoyne had friends in high places. While hunting, he handed a copy of his proposal to his companions, including King George III and Lord George Germain, the Secretary of State for the Colonies. Germain accepted the plan and wrote General Sir Guy Carleton on March 26, 1777, "You will be informed, by the contents thereof, that as soon as you should have driven the rebel forces from the frontiers of Canada, it was his Majesty's pleasure that you should return to Quebec, and take with you such part of your army as in your judgment and discretion appeared sufficient for the defence of the province; that you should detach Lieutenant General Burgoyne, or such other officer as you should think most proper, with the remainder of the troops, and direct the officer so detached to proceed with all possible expedition to join General Howe, and to put himself under his command. With a view of quelling the rebellion as soon as possible, it is become highly necessary that the most speedy junction of the two armies should be effected; and therefore, as the security and good government of Canada absolutely require your presence there, it is the King's determination to leave about 3000 men under your command, for the defence and duties of that province, and to employ the remainder of your army upon two expeditions, the one under the command of Lieutenant General Burgoyne, who is to force his way to Albany, and the other under the command of Lieutenant Colonel St. Leger, who is to make a diversion on the Mohawk River. As this plan cannot be advantageously executed without the assistance of Canadians and Indians, his Majesty strongly recommends it to your care, to furnish both expeditions with good and sufficient bodies of those men; and I am happy in knowing that your influence among them is so great, that there can be no room to apprehend you will find it difficult to fulfil his Majesty's expectations."

Germain

Carleton

As direct as Germain's orders to Carleton were, one critical individual was left out of the loop. That, unfortunately for the success of the entire operation, was General Howe. Richard Ketchum described the circumstances that left Howe completely in the dark concerning his role in Burgoyne's plan. Howe did receive a copy of the letter to Carleton, but nothing more specific: "According to William Knox, one of Germain's undersecretaries, his lordship was on his way to the country when he stopped by the office to sign his mail and was remained that nothing had been written to Howe specifying what action was expected of him. Lord George was annoyed. His carriage was waiting, he did not want his horses to be kept standing, and his tolerance for frustration was just about nil. He made it clear that he had no intention of spending another minute at the office, so Mr. D'Oyly, who handled traffic concerning the war, said he would prepare an order for the general and enclose the copy of Germain's letter to Carleton...but since Howe later denied having received any instructions except the copy of the message to Carleton, it may be supposed that D'Oyly's 'order' was nothing of the kind but at most a note explaining the enclosure. Of considerably more importance than his 'missing dispatch' is what Lord George neglected to tell Sir William. Given Germain's proclivity for giving his field commanders minutely detailed orders...it is incomprehensible that between March 3 and April 19--a period of seven weeks--he wrote eight letters to Howe and never once referred to the Burgoyne expedition or to what was expected from Howe in the way of cooperation. This meant that Howe's total knowledge of the joint operation was as described in Germain's letter to Carleton...If Howe failed to understand the purpose of the invasion from Canada, as he later claimed, Germain had no one but himself to blame."

Instead, Howe would turn his forces against Philadelphia, an operation that Burgoyne was not aware of himself. The success of Burgoyne's entire operation depended on linking up with a force that was not going to be there, and Burgoyne would not know this until it was too late.

The delicate job of delivering Germain's instructions to General Carleton was Burgoyne's. He sailed with Germain's letter from Portsmouth, England, on a ship bound for New York on March 28, 1777. Arriving in New York after a cruise of some weeks, he transferred to the frigate *Apollo* and supervised the loading of his personal baggage, which included an ample supply of champagne, claret, and brandy. After a wait of nearly six weeks, Burgoyne landed along the cliffs of Quebec on May 6, 1777. 10 days later, Burgoyne arrived at Montreal and took command of the British forces in Canada.

The British forces under Burgoyne's new command that were to participate in his invasion of New York had been resupplied and retrained after repelling the American invasion of Quebec, another campaign headed in part by Arnold, in early 1776. The British lacked enough horses, however, and that hampered their operations.

About 3,700 men under Burgoyne were British regulars, many of whom were veterans of Quebec or had fought at Lexington, Concord, and Bunker Hill. There were about an equal number of German mercenaries. To move his men, Carleton had assembled 500 flat-bottomed boats, along with the gunboats and sailing vessels he had constructed to repel the Americans. Burgoyne also brought with him 138 artillery pieces, ranging from three pounders to large 24 pounders, along with 450 artillerymen to man them. Under Burgoyne were Major General William Phillips, leading the British forces, and Major General Friedrich Baron von Riedesel, leading the German forces.

Baron von Riedesel

Once the forces assembled, the expedition left Canada on June 13, 1777. In a letter to a friend, a young officer accompanying Burgoyne's expedition provided a vivid description of the British forces on the march: "I cannot forbear portraying to your imagination one of the most pleasing spectacles I ever beheld. When we were in the widest part of the lake, whose beauty and extent I have already described, it was remarkably fine and clear, not a breeze was stirring, when the whole army appeared at one view in such perfect regularity as to form the most complete and splendid regatta you can possibly conceive. In the front the Indians went with their birch-bark canoes, containing twenty or thirty each; then the advanced corps in regular line with the gun-boats, then followed the Royal George and Inflexible, towing large booms — which are to be thrown across two points of land — with the two brigs and sloops following; after them Generals Burgoyne, Phillips and Riedesel in their pinnaces; next to them the second Battalion, followed by the German Battalion; and the rear was brought up with the sutlers and followers of the army. Upon the appearance of so formidable a fleet you may imagine they were not a little dismayed at Ticonderoga, for they were appraised of our advance, as we every day could see their watch-boats."

Throughout the campaign, Burgoyne counted on assistance from Loyalists and the Native American tribes in New York to supplement his forces. However, as David Ellis noted, Burgoyne's assumptions proved wrong: "The Canadians, they hoped, would volunteer out of gratitude for British help in repelling the American invasion of the previous year. But only 150 Canadians appeared. In 1775 the French-speaking Canadians had shown little desire to fight Yankee invaders, and obviously had even less interest in marching hundreds of miles south to put down a rebellion. New York had probably the highest proportion of Loyalists or Tories of the thirteen Colonies. Moreover, most Iroquois of the Six Nations followed Joseph Brant, the Mohawk chief. Burgoyne hoped for great and from these two groups. A few Tories from Vermont and New York drifted into his camp. They did give him precise information about the frontier settlements and the roads but they added very little fighting strength...Indian scouts were indispensible as the eyes and ears of any expedition pushing its way through the wilderness. Burgoyne had hoped that as many as 1,000 warriors would join his force, but only some 400 showed up."

Bennington

While Burgoyne was preparing to march into New York and, he hoped, crush the American rebellion once and for all, the Americans were preparing for such an invasion. The northern division of the Continental Army was led by General Philip Schuyler, appointed by Congress in May to "absolute command over every part of the Northern Department." Ellen Walworth explained, "On the 3d of June he arrived in Albany and resumed his command. During his absence little had been done to carry forward his plans of defence, or to increase the little army that garrisoned the widely separated posts of the command. The Mohawk valley, always an object of especial care and solicitude to Schuyler, had been wholly neglected. Upon his arrival in Albany he immediately wrote to General Herki mer to hold the militia of Tryon county in readiness to repel any attack from the west; and he renewed his efforts to quiet and conciliate the Indians of the Six Nations, with whom he had great influence."

Schuyler

When informed of Burgoyne's movements, Schuyler inferred, correctly, that the British were aiming to take back Fort Ticonderoga, though he incorrectly assumed that the movement was a feint to mask a thrust against New England. Thus, he worked to strengthen Ticonderoga's defenses, and on June 12, 1777, Schuyler appointed Major General Arthur St. Clair to take command of the fort. Schuyler appealed to Washington for reinforcements, asked for assistance from the governments of Massachusetts and Connecticut, and attempted to gather the New York militia. Washington, however, was concerned that Burgoyne's moves were designed to draw him away from Philadelphia, leaving it open to General Howe's forces. Walworth explained, "It is evident that the situation of the Northern Department constantly occupied the attention of the Commander-in-Chief. When he was assured that Howe was in the capes of the Delaware, and there was no further doubt that Philadelphia was the point of attack, although himself in great need of troops and efficient officers, he parted with Morgan's Corps of five hundred picked men, and sent Arnold, of whose 'abilities as a General he entertained a high opinion, to assist the Army of the North. He also directed General Lincoln, then in New England, to repair to Schuyler's command, and advised that he should attempt a flank movement upon Burgoyne toward the east. He also addressed circulars to the Brigadier-Generals of Militia in Western Massachusetts and Connecticut, urging them to march with a large part of their command to Saratoga, or other rendezvous designated by General Schuyler. To the latter he wrote, warning him against collecting large quantities of ammunition and other stores in forts and lines of defense. 'I begin to consider lines,' he writes, 'a kind of trap, unless they are in passes which cannot be avoided by the enemy.'…The scantiness of the garrison, the contentions among its commanders, and the final unexpected rapidity of Burgoyne's advance, may partly explain the apparent want of sound military judgement that caused this fortress to fall like ripe fruit into the hands of the invader."

St. Clair

Daniel Morgan

Due to a series of miscommunications, Ticonderoga would prove more vulnerable than the rebels anticipated. Schuyler had appointed Anthony Wane to command Fort Ticonderoga, which had a garrison of over 2,000 men, on November 18, 1776. Shortly after he arrived, Wayne wrote General Schuyler, "DEAR GENERAL,-I herewith send you a Return of this Garrison as also of the Soldiers re-engaged to serve during the War—which are but few— "Liberty to come down for one month when Relieved" carries with it an Idea of being Immediately sent back again to a place which they Imagine to be very unhealthy;—they say; march us off this Ground and then we will Cheerfully Re-engage; add to this their anxiety about their friends in the Jerseys and Penns'a makes them Impatient to be led to the assistance of their Distressed Country They likewise see the Eastern people Running away in the Clouds of the Night—(some before and all soon as their times expires). Col Whitcombs Regiment—all the Sailors & Mariners—the whole of the Artificers and all the Corps of Artillery except Capt. Roman's Company (which consists but of 12 men Officers Included) are gone off the Ground Notwithstanding so bad an example—and the distress of their native State—the Pennsylvanians, will not leave me until fresh troops arrive to Relieve them Your own feelings Sir on the Alarming Situation of Affairs in Penns'a and Jersey; will best Inform you of that of every Other Officer and Soldier (from those States) on the Present Occasion: which causes us most Ardently to wish for an Opportunity of meeting those Sons of War and Rapine—face to face; and man to man. These worthy fellows are Second to none in Courage (I have seen them proved)—and I know that they are not far behind any Regulars in Point of Discipline— Such troops, actuated by Principle, and fired with just Resentment must be an Acceptable, and perhaps season able Reinforcement to Gen'l Washington at this Critical Juncture— If you shou'd be of the same Opinion and cause us to be Immediately relieved—with Orders to march with all Dispatch to join the main Army—I believe we shou'd be able to Re-enlist the Chief part of our people on the way: however this may be I wou'd answer for it that they will not turn aside from Danger (altho their terms shou'd be expired) when the safety and Honor of their Country Require them to face it— I must Once more earnestly Request you to Order up shoes and soap—we are much Distressed for want of these Necessary Articles— Doct'r M'Crea arrived last night with some Medicine—but Hospital Stores, roots and Vegetables we are totally Destitute of."

A short time later, Wayne appraised Schuyler of the situation of the fort, which he wrote of in stark terms while complimenting the troops under his command: "DEAR GEN'L,-Col Simons Reg't Col Robinsons Reg't Consisting of about 700 men Officers Included are now Arrived together with 24 men of Col Warner's Regiment— In Consequence I have Ordered One Reg't of the Penns'a to march tomorrow. The Others will follow as soon as Possible with Orders to Proceed in Good Order to Phil'a— I have Lately Rec'd letters from Gen'l St. Clair and other Gent'm in Gen'l Washing ton's Camp which made me think it Advisable to keep these Regt's Embodied until they are Dismissed by the Board of War:—their time expired the 5th of this Instant: they are to be settled within Phil'a agreeable to Promise, when I have Reason to expect the greatest part will Reengage— I want much to go also—it would be in my Power to do more with them in case of necessity than perhaps any other Officer: I know these worthy fellows well and they know me— I am Confident they would not Desert me in a time of Danger— If you think it would be for the benefit of the Service—I shou'd be glad to be Immediately Relieved in Command with Orders to march with the last of the Southern troops. For the present I am using every Effort to Render this place strong. I shall soon Complete the Abattis Round the Old fort, and Octagons on Mt. Independence, and two New Blockhouses; so that in a few days we hope to Render this post tenable and leave it in a much securer and better state than we found it—the manner in which I have kept our Guards and Sentries and the Constant Succession of Scouts which I have out—if followed by my successor—will Effect ually prevent a surprise; you will please to Order the Other troops Destin'd for this Garrison to be forward'd with all Possible Dispatch"

In February 1777, Wayne wrote to his friend Sharp Delany, "I must now in Confidence tell you that this post has been most shamefully neglected—all the old and good Troops are gone—none here but a few wretched militia—badly armed and worse Disciplined— This Garrison at this time Ought to Consist of at least 5000 Effective men—with a well trained Corps of Artillery—perhaps Congress thinks it does. I have not One fifth part of that number on the Ground—and I would much Rather Risque my life, Reputation, and the fate of America on 400 Good Troops, than the Whole of the present Garrison. This is the Situation of the Second post in the United States— the Neighboring Governments are now roused—and I expect in a few days to be strongly Re-enforced— A body of the Enemy were Discovered a few days since marching this way by two Canadians— who are gone to Albany—this has awaked Gen'l Schuyler and Others (whose business it was to send Troops) from their Lethargy— We may probably have some Diversion in a few Hours—I have yet some good men on whom I can Depend—and I will be answerable for the maintenance of this post until succour can Arrive."

An engraving of Wayne

Delany

Although Wayne wrote pessimistically about the conditions at Ticonderoga in letters to acquaintances, he was still confident that the position could not be taken by the British without a bloody fight, and he expressed that to his superiors. In part because of that confidence, Wayne would be ordered to leave the fort in early 1777 to help Washington elsewhere.

That ended up weakening Ticonderoga months before Burgoyne's forces landed at Crown Point, 10 miles north of Ticonderoga, in late June 1777. There, on June 30, Burgoyne issued an order to his men: "The Army embarks tomorrow to approach the Enemy. We are to contend for the King and the Constitution of Great Britain, to vindicate the Law and to relieve the Oppressed. A Cause in which His Majesty's Troops and those of the Princes His Allies, will feel equal Excitement. The Services required of this particular Expedition are critical and conspicuous. During our progress occasions may occur, in which nor difficulty nor labour nor lise are to be regarded. This Army must not Retreat."

Burgoyne advanced towards Ticonderoga, capturing Mount Hope, the mills at the outlet of Lake George, and Sugar Hill on July 4. Under the cover of darkness, Burgoyne's forces moved their artillery into place, and on the morning of July 5, St. Clair and the Americans could see the British busy at work constructing an artillery battery on Mount Defiance, 700 feet above Fort Ticonderoga. The Americans had long been aware of Mount Defiance's commanding position, but nobody had bothered to man it or defend it, wrongly assuming the British could not haul artillery up there. However, as British Major General William Phillips succinctly put it, "Where a goat can go, a man can go; and where a man can go, he can drag a gun."

Seeing no alternative but to evacuate the position once the British manned Fort Defiance, St. Clair quietly ordered an orderly retreat under the guise of making a sortie against the British forces. Over the next couple of days, the American forces managed to escape. Burgoyne came into possession of Fort Ticonderoga, but he had not crushed the enemy as he had hoped.

A picture of Fort Ticonderoga from Mount Defiance

Burgoyne reported the capture of Ticonderoga to Germain in a letter dated July 11, 1777: "I HAVE the honour to inform your Lordship, that the enemy, dislodged from Ticonderoga and Mount Independant, on the 6th instant, and were driven, on the same day, beyond Skenesborough on the right, and to Humerton on the left, with the loss of 128 pieces of cannon, all their armed vessels and bateaux, the greatest part of their baggage and ammunition, provision, and military stores, to a very large amount. This success has been followed by events equally fortunate and rapid. I subjoin such a detail of circumstances as the time will permit; and for his Majesty's further information, I beg leave to refer your Lordship to Captain Gardner, my aid de camp, whom I thought it necessary to dispatch with news so important to the King's service and so honourable to the troops under my command."

Although it was a clear British victory, as they had on repeated occasions, the American forces survived to fight another day. The remnants of St. Clair's command made their way through the forests of northern New York to meet up with Schuyler's force at Albany, and many of them would be on hand to fight around Saratoga.

After hearing that St. Clair had evacuated Ticonderoga. Schuyler thought the worst and was relieved when St. Clair and his tired and haggard force arrived at Fort Edward. Walworth described of the mood in the American camp: "These misfortunes in the beginning of the campaign involved a heavy loss of artillery, small arms, and stores of all kinds; the consternation of the people who fled before Burgoyne seemed still more disastrous, and Schuyler's fortitude and composure were most severely tried. He was sustained and encouraged by constant dispatches from Washington, who writes at one time, 'We should never despair. If new difficulties arise we must only put forth new exertions,' and again he expresses an earnest sympathy for Schuyler amid these thickening difficulties, and manifests his unwavering confidence in his ability to overcome them. With unflagging energy Schuyler exerted himself to delay the enemy while endeavoring to collect a sufficient force to meet him with some reasonable prospect of success."

Schuyler remained at Fort Edward until his forces had blocked the passages from Skenesborough, where Burgoyne lingered at camp. Walworth noted, "Huge stones were rolled into Wood Creek, and trees felled across it; bridges were destroyed, and the forests leveled across the roads. The surrounding country was stripped of forage and the cattle driven off, so that the enemy would be compelled to rely upon his base of operations for provisions."

These obstacles forced Burgoyne to have men spend about two weeks cutting a road for his heavy artillery from Skenesboro to Fort Edward. Naturally, by the time Burgoyne's forces reached Fort Edward, Schuyler's forces were gone.

In the wake of yet another retreat, the morale of American forces had reached a low ebb. The constant retreats made the men uneasy about their own leaders and uncertain of their own fighting capacity. Dozens of men deserted the army each day, to the extent that by August 1, only about 4,000 men were left, many of whom were boys, old men, and black servants.

The Americans needed a rallying cry, and it would soon arrive.

In the vicinity of Fort Edward lived a Tory widow, Sarah McNeil, who awaited the arrival of her cousin, General Simon Fraser, who was with Burgoyne's forces. Living with McNeil was a young woman, a beautiful 23-year-old named Jane McCrea. McCrea herself was waiting for her fiancé, a local boy named David Jones who had run away to Canada to serve with the British. On July 27, McNeil arrived at Burgoyne's camp in the company of two of the British side's native allies, alleging that Jane had been killed and scalped by the two. In his journal of the campaign, Lieutenant William Digby wrote about the incident, "In the evening, our Indians brought in two scalps, one of them an officer's which they danced about in their usual manner. Indeed, the cruelties committed by them, were too shocking to relate, particularly the melancholy catastrophe of the unfortunate Miss McCrea, which affected the general and the whole army with the sincerest regret and concern for her untimely fate. This young lady was about 18, had a pleasing person, her family were loyal to the King, and she engaged to be married to a provincial officer, in our Army, before the war broke out. Our Indians (I may well now call them Savages) were detached on scouting parties, both in out front and on our flanks, and came to the house where she resided; but the scene is too tragic for my pen. She fell a sacrifice to the savage passions of these blood thirsty monsters...I make no doubt, but the censorious world, who seldom judge but by outward appearances, will be apt to censure General Burgoyne for the cruelties committed by his Indians, and imagine he countenanced them in so acting. On the contrary, I am pretty certain it was always against his desire to give any assistance to the savages."

Fraser

When word of McCrea's death arrived at General Horatio Gates' headquarters, he wrote Burgoyne, "That the savages of America should in their warfare mangle and scalp the unhappy prisoners, who fall into their hands, is neither new nor extraordinary; but that the famous Lieut General Burgoyne, in whom the fine gentleman is united with the soldier and the scholar, should hire the savages of America to scalp Europeans and the descendants of Europeans; nay more that he should pay a price for each scalp so barbarously taken, is more than will be believed in England until authenticated facts shall in every gazette convince mankind of the truth of this horrid tale.— Miss McCrea, a young lady lovely to the sight, of virtuous character and amiable disposition, engaged to be married to an officer in your army, was with other women and children taken out of a house near Fort Edward, carried into the woods, and there scalped and mangled in the most shocking manner. Two parents with their six children, [were] all treated with the same inhumanity while quietly residing in their once happy and peaceful dwelling. The miserable fate of Miss McCrea was partly aggravated by her being dressed to receive her promised husband; but met her murderers employed by you. Upwards of one hundred men, women and children have perished by the hands of these ruffians, to whom it is asserted, you have paid the price of blood."

Burgoyne replied, "It has happened, that all my transactions with the Indian nations last year and this, have been open, clearly heard, distinctly understood and accurately minuted by very numerous, and in many parts, very prejudiced audiences. So diametrically opposite to truth is your assertion that I have paid a price for scalps, that one of the first regulations established by me at the great Council in May, and repeated and enforced, and invariably adhered to since, was that the Indians should receive compensation for prisoners, because it would prevent cruelty, and that not only such compensations should be withheld, but a strict account demanded for scalps. These pledges of Conquest— for such you well know they will ever esteem them — were solemnly and peremptorily prohibited to be taken from the wounded and even the dying, and the persons of aged men, women and children, and prisoners were pronounced sacred even, in assaults. Respecting Miss McCrea; her fall wanted not the tragic display you have laboured to give it, to make it as sincerely abhorred and lamented by me, as it can possibly be by the tenderest of her friends. The fact was no premeditated barbarity, on the contrary, two chiefs who had brought her off for the purpose of security, not of violence to her person, disputed who should be her guard, and in a fit of savage passion in the one from whose hands she was snatched, the unhappy woman became the victim. Upon the first intelligence of the events, I obliged the Indians to deliver the murderer into my hands, and tho to have punished him by our laws and principles of justice would have been perhaps unprecedented, he certainly should have suffered an ignominious death, had I not been convinced, by circumstances and observation beyond the possibility of a doubt, that a pardon under the terms I prescribed and they accepted, would be more efficacious than an execution to prevent similar mischiefs. The above instance excepted, your intelligence respecting cruelties of the Indians. is absolutely false. You seem to threaten me with European publications, which affect me as little as any other threats you could make, but in regard to American publications, whether the charge against me, (which I acquit you of believing), was pencilled from a gazette or for a gazette, I desire and demand of you, as a man of honour, that should it appear in print at all, this answer may follow it."

Gates

In spite of Burgoyne's protests, the American press publicized McCrea's death as an example of the barbarity of the British, not just their native allies. David Wilson wrote in *The Life of Jane McCrea*, published in 1853, "The account of this dreadful tragedy at once circulated far and wide over the land, and everywhere excited the liveliest emotions of sympathy. By every fireside, in public assemblies, in the national counsels, it was told and re-told, until the story of Jane McCrea was known throughout the continent. It was the subject of songs and ballads. It crossed the Atlantic, and was caught up by those who had opposed the war. In the House of Commons, while denouncing the ministry for having employed savages in the struggle against the Colonies, Burke repeated it with all the vehemence arid power that characterized his glowing eloquence. It spread still farther, through France, Germany, Italy, and over all the nations of Europe that recognized the rules of civilized warfare; and the inhumanity of England in making allies of barbarians who could be guilty of such atrocious and cruel acts, was everywhere condemned. Among the patriots, the murder of the defenseless girl, excited emotions of unappeasable indignation."

The indignation prompted hundreds of men to flock to the militia to join the fight against Burgoyne's invasion.

The Death of Jane McCrea **by John Vanderlyn (1804)**

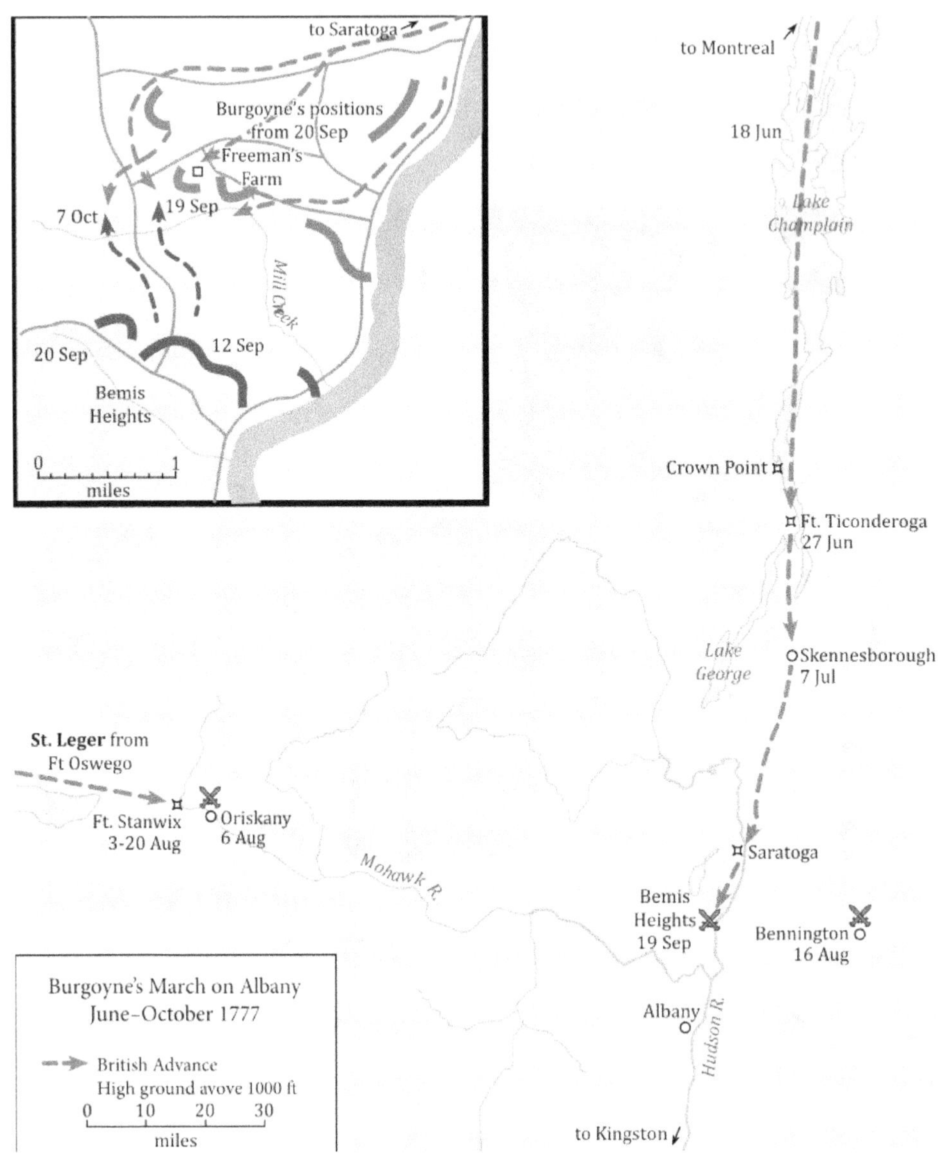

A map of the armies' movements toward Saratoga

By this point, Burgoyne was beginning to have bigger problems than simply the rising anger of the Americans against the British and their native allies. One of the most famous military maxims attributed to Napoleon is that an army marches on its stomach, and to say the logistics of supplying British forces proved difficult would be an understatement. Given the fact that supply lines were dependent on Canada and England, supplying Burgoyne's forces would be just as difficult as executing a massive invasion of the colonies.

Indeed, by the time the first phase of his envisioned campaign had ended, Burgoyne faced a dilemma. In his history of the battle, Richard Ketchum noted that Burgoyne "had not the slightest doubt that his army would overrun the rebels and reach Albany, but his decision to sit tight at Skenesborough was based on a number of considerations. Nor was the time the realities of a wilderness campaign conducted far from a base hit home like a blow to the stomach, and what had seemed simple when he studied his options on a map in London began to take on a daunting complexity. The army's real base of operations was Canada, and although depts, or magazines as they were called, had been established along the way...the round trip for ships sailing back and forth was painfully slow, even with no enemy vessels to oppose them. The business of furnishing food, ammunition, and other necessities for a force of some seven thousand men plus women, camp followers, and heaven only knew how many animals was beginning to assume awesome proportions if for no reason other than the length of the supply line and the time it took for an essential item to travel from Montreal or Quebec to Skenesborough or beyond. The general dared not order his entire army to march until he was satisfied that he had an adequate store of everything on hand and a fully operative, reliable system for supplying the army's needs on a regular basis." Given these problems, Ketchum pointed out that Burgoyne "could not know it, but the days of rapid forward movement and lightning successes were over."

While Burgoyne's advance on Albany stalled, another British force was marching into New York from Canada from the west. A force of 300 British regulars and 650 Canadian and Loyalist militia led by Lieutenant Colonel Barry St. Leger crossed Lake Ontario and took Oswego without incident. There, St. Leger's force was joined by 1,000 natives.

St. Leger

From Oswego, St. Leger's force marched on July 25 to Fort Stanwix, and the British began to lay siege to that fort on August 2. A force of American militia and their native allies led by General Nicholas Herkimer marched to relieve the siege, but they were ambushed by the British and their native allies on August 6 at Oriskany. Henry Cookinham explained, "At the ravine in the dense forest, two miles beyond the Oriskany Creek, were concealed some 500 British soldiers, Canadians and Tories, and as many Indians under the great leader, Thayendanegea. Unconscious of danger, the patriots passed along the rough woods road into the ravine. Suddenly a thousand rifles cracked. The air about them was filled with smoke, and the yells of the Indians reverberated through the forest. Surprised — appalled — staggered — the 800 patriots were thrown into confusion. But their commander did not lose his self control, and, with courage unsurpassed, he rallied his men and sent back a well directed fire. Early in the conflict General

Herkimer was wounded, and then, seated upon the ground, with courage, than which none is greater, he directed the battle to the end. The fierceness of this struggle was never surpassed in modern warfare. Of the 800 patriots who participated in the fight, less than 200 remained unscathed when the retreat began after the battle was over. The loss upon the side of the enemy, as reported by St. Leger, was 300, but this, probably, does not include the loss among the Indians, which was very great, as Joseph Brant, Thayendanegea, many times after referred to the suffering of his poor Mohawks in this conflict. During the battle there was a sortie from Fort Stanwix led by Colonel Willett, the second in command, and it was most successful in capturing the camp of Sir John Johnson, a vast amount of property, and the order book of Sir John."

On August 10, a force of 800 men led by Benedict Arnold left Stillwater, New York and marched toward Fort Stanwix. Arriving at Fort Dayton on August 21, Arnold was only able to recruit a further 100 militia men to continue the march. Resorting to subterfuge, Arnold released a Loyalist prisoner with information tricking St. Leger into thinking that Arnold's force was much larger than it actually was. Upon receiving this news, St. Leger's native allies withdrew from Fort Stanwix, taking the remaining supplies with them. Left in the New York wilderness without adequate supplies, St. Leger was forced to abandon the siege of the fort and lead his hungry men back to Quebec.

With that, Burgoyne's campaign, which relied on a three-pronged thrust, was down to a one-pronged thrust. Burgoyne would only begin to realize this when a messenger from General Howe arrived at Fort Edward on August 3, bringing a letter written on July 17: "I have received yours of the second instant on the 15th, have since heard from the rebel army of your being in possession of Ticonderoga, which is a great event, carried without loss. I have received your two letters, viz. from Plymouth and Quebec, your last of the 14th May, and shall observe the contents. There is a report of a messenger of yours to me having been taken, and the letter discovered in a double wooden canteen, you will know if it was of any consequence; nothing of it has transpired to us. I will observe the same rules in writing to you, as you propose, in your letters to me. Washington is waiting our motions here, and has detached Sullivan with about 2500 men, as I learn, to Albany. My intention is for Pennsylvania, where I expect to meet Washington, but if he goes to the northward contrary to my expectations, and you can keep him at bay, be assured I shall soon be after him to relieve you. After your arrival at Albany, the movements of the enemy will guide yours; but my wishes are, that the enemy be drove out of this province before any operation takes place in Connecticut. Sir Henry Clinton remains in the command here, and will act as occurrences my direct. Putnam is in the highlands with about 4000 men."

This was obviously not good news for Burgoyne. Not only would Howe's forces not be available to reinforce his troops at Albany, but this meant Howe could not be relied on to bring additional supplies for Burgoyne's forces. Concerned that the supply situation was only going to become more serious, Burgoyne decided to act on a suggestion of Baron von Riedesel had made in July to send a force east towards the New Hampshire Grants and Western Massachusetts (present day Vermont) to forage for supplies and capture draft animals and other resources to supplement the British. Thus, Burgoyne sent Colonel Fredrich Baum's regiment to that area, but on August 16, Baum's forces were met by a force of New Hampshire militia led by John Stark at Bennington. Samuel Bartlett would later write of the ensuing battle, "The morning of the sixteenth opened in absolute beauty. Not a cloud. Not a stirring leaf. Raindrops glittered 'like diamonds' in the trees. The river alone seemed alive as it rolled along 'swollen and tumultuous.' The German officer never forgot that beautiful scene. For hours not an enemy had been seen nor a sound of alarm had been heard. All was so peaceful that the leaders grew confident, and breakfast was ordered preparatory to action. But it was the hush of the crouching catamount. Scarcely were the haversacks unslung and the muskets piled when the men were called in all haste to their ranks. The same officer, Glich, looking out from his zigzag breastwork on the hill, to his amazement saw the pickets retiring, the outposts withdrawing, and a strange body of men emerging from the thicket behind. He watched in alarm as they marched and counter marched conspicuously in sight. Two of their officers rode forth to reconnoiter; and as the British cannonier fired his harmless shot he did not know that he aimed at Warner and Stark. Suddenly Glich heard a trampling behind in the forest on the right. It was Herrick and his Rangers in their uniform of green. Then came a shout and a rattling fire in the rear on the left. It was Nichols, of Amherst, giving the signal to begin. From before sunrise they had wound in single file through the forest, and now with a green twig in every hatband they came forth. Scarcely had the sound of the first fire died out when the Indians broke and fled. A column pushed forward on the tory breastwork on this side of the river. It was Stickney and Hobart, and for a badge every man had a corn husk in his hat. At the same signal the main body moved up in front and the battle raged on every side…and as they climbed the slippery steep behind them came rolling down beneath the shots of our marksmen. For two hours, from three to five o 'clock, the fire was one continuous roar. Those death dealing columns closed in nearer and nearer. At eight paces distance they picked off the canonniers from their guns. Still nearer they came until the flashes met. The ammunition cart exploded within the entrenchments, and at the sound our men rushed up, scaled the breastworks, and leaped down within. Then came a terrible clashing of sword and gunstock and bayonet. Gigantic John McNeil struck down four Hessians with the butt of his gun. In five minutes twenty men broke through to the forest. The rest were all prisoners or dead or dying. They fought gallantly and their leader died a soldier's death."

Total German and British losses at Bennington were recorded at 207 dead and 700 captured, while American losses included 30 dead and 40 wounded. The American victory at Bennington, when combined with the death of Jane McCrea, proved a rallying cry for the patriots, and the fighting also soured relations between Burgoyne and his native and Canadian allies. As a result, most of the native allies abandoned Burgoyne's camp, leaving his force with little protection from American rangers who lurked in the surrounding forests and harassed his men. Burgoyne's position was increasingly challenging.

Stark

Freeman's Farm

While Burgoyne's invasion had stalled, Congress was still full of panic in Philadelphia, and the chief beneficiary of these concerns was Horatio Gates. Congress was shocked by the fall of Ticonderoga, and Gates voiced concerns about generals reluctant to confront the enemy head on. While referring to Schuyler, Gates was also inferentially referring to Washington. At this time, Washington's main concern was preserving the Continental Army as a fighting force, and given the odds, the commander-in-chief carefully avoided a direct confrontation with the British unless there was clear numerical superiority. Some in Congress had grown impatient with this strategy; yearning for a decisive battle that would win the country's independence outright, despite the fact the Continental Army lacked the numbers, training, and resources to defeat the most professional army in the world.

As a result, in response to Ticonderoga and Gates' assertions, Congress overrode the objections of the New York delegation and appointed Gates commander of the Northern Department on August 10. Arriving in Albany on August 19, Gates quickly alienated Schuyler, who soon departed for Philadelphia.

Throughout August and September, militia companies from Pennsylvania and Massachusetts joined the Continental Army along the Hudson, and Washington ordered troops under Arnold to augment Gates' forces. These men were rallied to the cause by the outrage over Jane McCrea's death and the successes at Bennington and Fort Stanwix. These forces swelled Gates' ranks to over 6,000 men by the middle of September, which rivaled Burgoyne's numbers.

Walworth summarized Burgoyne's actions leading up to the Battle of Saratoga: "The defeat of Baum, and the failure of St. Leger, by successive strokes, had paralyzed the right and the left arms of Burgoyne's force, and he now struggled forward with the maimed body of his army, amid ever thickening danger. Yet undismayed, he assiduously endeavored to carry out his original design, and obey the orders of Germaine and the King. Having collected provisions for a thirty days' march, he dispatched a messenger to New York with entreaties for a movement to be made from that direction. He then left Duer's House, and moved his army steadily forward to the Batten Kill, where he encamped on the night of the twelfth of September. Finding that his officers were reluctant to cross the river, he assumed the entire responsibility himself, and on the 13th and 14th passed the whole army over the Hudson on a bridge of boats, enforcing his order, " This army must not retreat." They continued their march down the river, and encamped on the northside of Fish Creek. Here, in sight of Old Saratoga, which lay on the southside of the stream, closed the second period of the campaign," and with dramatic propriety the curtain falls upon another act, which in its progress has. already indicated the direction of coming events. Here also, on the night of the 14th of September, Burgoyne's encampment rested on the very spot where, a few weeks later, his surrender took place. This place was several miles above the battle-field of Bemis Heights. From a hill on the east side of the Hudson, Colonel Colburn, of the Continental Army, reconnoitred this camp. Perched in the forks of a tall tree, he counted through his field-glass eight hundred tents; watched the army prepare for and start on its forward march, and then hastened to Stillwater to make his report to Gates."

Burgoyne's orders betrayed his growing anxiety amid his determination to press onward with his plan of attack. On September 14 he told his men, "During the next marches of the army, the corps are to move in such a state as to be fit for instant action. It is a standing order for the rest of the campaign, that all pickets and guards are under arms an hour before daylight, and remain so until it is completely light." The next day, he said, "The army are to march in three columns, after having passed Schuyler's house — The provisions to be floated down under the care of Captain Brown — The hospitals to move as quick as carts can be provided for them — The bridge to be broke up and floated down immediately after the army is marched."

By September 18, advanced units of his army reached a position just north of Saratoga, only four miles from the American lines. What Burgoyne did not know, in the absence of reliable Indian scouting, was that Gates was waiting for him in force to the south of Saratoga. On September 8, Gates had ordered his army, which had ballooned to about 10,000 men, to march to Stillwater to set up a defensive position there. His engineer, Tadeusz Kościuszko, decided that the town itself was not defensible, so the Pole chose Bemis Heights, four miles above Stillwater, as the most favorable position. Gates' army soon set up camp at that place and construction began on a line of defensive entrenchments.

Kościuszko

Within a period of a week, Kościuszko altered the earthworks and positioned heavy weaponry into a strong array of defenses, and Walworth described the American position: "The position chosen for the American camp, where Gates had determined to await an attack, was on a spur of hills that approached the river bank. At their base, on the river, stood Bemis' house, used by Gates as head-quarters for a few days; he afterwards moved on the hill. Earthworks were thrown across the narrow meadow between the hill and the river; they covered the old road., and the bridge of boats communicating with the east side of the Hudson. The heights were to the north and west. Breastworks were projected toward the north, in a semi-circle, for three-quarters of a mile. Redoubts were established at intervals. A barn built of heavy logs, belonging to the Neilson farm, which lay within the works, was converted into a rude but strong fortification. A thickly wooded ravine formed a natural defense along the front of the camp, and Mill Creek swept through a deeper ravine, a little to the north. Gates occupied, with the right wing, the river hills and the defile between these and the river; Morgan, of Arnold's division, the left wing, camped on the heights nearly a mile back from the river, and Learned occupied the elevated plain as centre."

Gates took command of the American right, to the east, while he put Arnold in command of the army's left, on the western part of Bemis Heights. Arnold's troops, numbering some 1,500 men, skirmished with Burgoyne's forces constantly, forcing the British general to assign a whole regiment to guard a small working party. Arnold soon alienated Gates, however, when he chose friends of Schuyler to staff his command. This immediately led to tensions between the two generals.

On the morning of September 19, Burgoyne advanced towards the Americans in three columns, with Baron von Riedesel commanding the left, Burgoyne taking the center, and Fraser moving far to the west. Burgoyne's aim was for Fraser's force and his force to unite in the rear of the left wing of the American camp, hoping that while the Canadians and Indians distracted the American forces in the front, Fraser would get into the rear of the Americans. Burgoyne would simultaneously attack the front and Riedesel would occupy Gates on the American right.

Gates learned of the British approach, but he still delayed giving orders to meet the enemy. He finally yielded to Arnold's request to move his forces out to Freeman's Farm to anticipate the British move on the American left flank. Together with Daniel Morgan's riflemen, some of Arnold's light infantry advanced from their defensive position and met Fraser's forces approaching from the west.

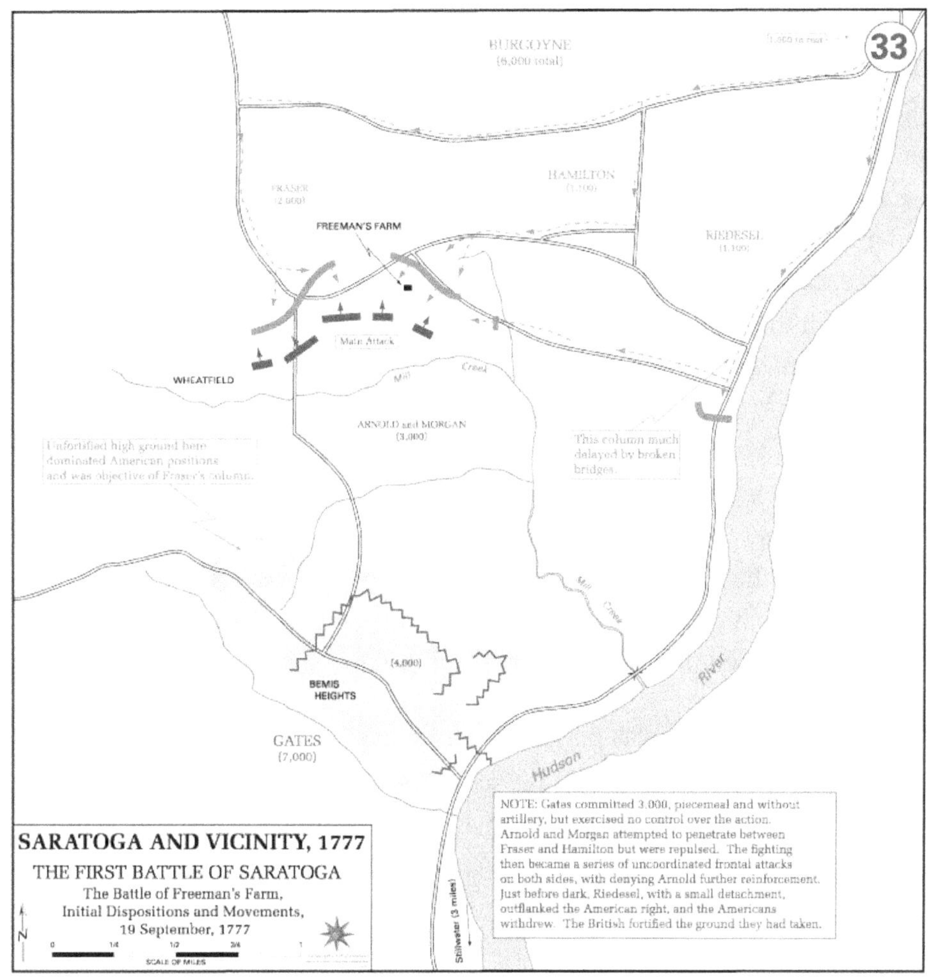

A map of the positions at Freeman's Farm

Walworth explained, "The American regiments behind their works were restless and eager for the contest, and no sooner were they permitted to move than they assailed the enemy with resistless impetuosity. Morgan led the way with his riflemen, who drove the advancing forces with such rapidity, that, for a moment, their commander lost sight of them. His shrill whistle soon recalled them to calmer work. Now following, Arnold with Learned's brigade, they attempted to cut off the detachment of Fraser from the main army; Fraser at the same time was endeavoring to reach the American rear. Both striving for the same object, and their movements screened by the heavy forest, they met unexpectedly near Mill Creek, a few yards west of Freeman's cottage. A furious contest followed. Arnold led with his usual spirit, while Morgan seemed endowed with the strength and ubiquity of a forest demi-god; with his active, intelligence corps, he struck blow after blow, his men scattering like leaves of the autumn before a gust of the British bayonets, only to close again and follow up their advantage. Assailing Breyman's guns, they captured a cannon, and were carrying it from the field when Morgan's horse was shot under him.; heavy reinforcements came to relieve Fraser; Gates still withheld assistance, and they were scattered once more. Arnold and Morgan now made a rapid counter march against Fraser's left, and in this movement encountered the whole English line under Burgoyne. They were now reinforced with four regiments, and made so vigorous and resolute an attack that they were on the point of severing the wings of the British army, when Phillips came forward with his artillery, and the Americans were forced back within their lines. It was now three o'clock, and a lull occurred in the contest. The two armies lay each upon a hillside, that sloped toward a ravine, which separated them. With the reinforcements conceded to Arnold, his force did not exceed three thousand men; yet, with this number, for four hours, he sustained an unequal conflict with the choicest English regiments, inspired by every sentiment that ambition or desperation could awaken, and commanded by many of the most accomplished and brave officers of the English Army. Steadily the Patriots received charge after charge of the dreaded English bayonets; then, emboldened by their own endurance, they pushed upon the enemy in a fierce attack, to be driven again toward their own lines. While victory seemed thus to sway back and forth over the little stream, which hid its crystal waters under the crimson flood that now crept over it, and while the Americans held the ascendancy, Riedesel came over the field at double-quick with his heavy Germans, and pressed the exhausted Americans back once more. It was now dark; they gathered up their wounded and prisoners and retired to their camp."

The Battle of Freeman's Farm was considered a British victory because they had succeeded in driving the Americans from the field, but it was a Pyrrhic victory at best. The American killed and wounded numbered about 300, but Burgoyne had lost almost 600 killed and wounded, representing nearly 10% of his force. Moreover, American forces kept up their harassment of his men, with small bands going out of the American lines to skirmish with the British on a continuous basis.

A view of the battlefield

Bemis Heights

With Burgoyne's position increasingly imperiled, the Americans could have attacked in force, but Gates resisted Arnold's increasingly vehement suggestions, resulting in a noisy argument in Gates' headquarters during which he told Arnold that his command was going to be given to General Benjamin Lincoln. Arnold requested leave to transfer to Washington's command, which Gates granted, but for reasons that are not entirely clear, Arnold remained in camp during this time. Gates also took Daniel Morgan's company and placed it under his direct command.

The British and American forces remained opposite each other from September 20-October 7 without barely moving camp. Walworth quoted one rebel soldier, who wrote, "Our army was exultant, hopeful; scarcely to be checked in its rest, less desire to drive the invader from the fruitful fields and deserted homes he desecrated and destroyed. Rushing out from their entrenchments under every plausible excuse to skirmish with the outposts of the enemy, or capture his pickets, the eager militia could with difficulty be restrained by the…cautious Gates from bringing on the general engagement that he seemed quite willing to avoid. The other camp seemed oppressed by the overhanging cloud of its impending fate. The British officers, perpetually on the alert, were unable to secure a single night of undisturbed repose; the men bore with quiet but sullen fortitude the privations and hardships of short rations, hurried snatches of sleep under full accoutrements, and constant calls to arms. More and more vivid to all grew the vision of that impassable wall of difficulties that enclosed them on all sides, leaving but one narrow pathway to the north."

Unbeknownst to Burgoyne, his route back to Canada had been cut off when American forces under General Lincoln and Colonel John Brown attacked the British at Ticonderoga. While unable to reduce the fort itself, the Americans did succeed in recapturing Skenesboro and Ticonderoga's outer defenses. Given Burgoyne's persistence in pressing the attack, it's doubtful that he would have abandoned his advance and retreated back to Canada even had he known about those developments.

All the while, he continued to hope for assistance from British forces to his south. He received a letter from General Sir Henry Clinton in New York on September 21 that offered the hope of such assistance in the form of a movement up the Hudson River to draw off Gates' army. Clinton told Burgoyne that he would attack the forts below the Highlands and attempt to move north. Burgoyne immediately dispatched two officers in disguise back to Clinton with a message describing the desperate state of his army and urging him to make haste. Furthermore, Burgoyne assured him that he would continue to hold his position until October 12.

As fate would have it, Clinton would actually begin moving forces that way and take some forts in the vicinity in early October, but his messengers announcing that to Burgoyne were captured. Thus, as the days passed without word from Clinton, and with the situation of his army becoming increasingly dire, Burgoyne decided he could not wait much longer for assistance from the south.

Burgoyne ultimately decided to take action on October 7, unaware that the American ranks had since swelled to nearly 15,000 men. Walworth noted, "As Burgoyne's situation became day by day more critical, and he received no news from Clinton, on the fourth of October he called Generals Riedesel, Phillips and Fraser together in council. Riedesel was strongly in favor of a retreat to Fort Edward, and Fraser conceded the wisdom of such a movement; Phillips declined to express an opinion, and Burgoyne finally declared that on the seventh he would make a reconnoissance, and if he then found the enemy too strong to be attacked, he would immediately retreat to Fort Edward, and await the cooperation of the army below. On the sixth he had five days' rations distributed, and arranged for a reconnaissance in force on the following day. As he could not leave his camp unprotected, he only took fifteen hundred men. They were selected from the corps of Riedesel, Fraser and Phillips. Led by these officers in person, and Burgoyne as Commander-in-Chief, they marched out of camp at eleven o'clock on the morning of the seventh, and entered a field within three-quarters of a mile of the American left. Here, in double ranks, they formed in line of battle. On the left Williams' artillery and Ackland's grenadiers were posted, on a gentle hill in the edge of a wood that fronted on Mill Creek. Balcarras' light infantry and other English regiments formed, the right: the Hessians held the centre. Fraser, with five hundred picked men, was posted to the right and front of Balcarras, where a hill skirted the meadow; he was ready to fall upon the rear of the American left at the first attack in front."

Unfortunately for Burgoyne's plan, the Americans soon divined the British intention to attack the left. Gates had sent soldiers into a field to forage for wheat, and these men spotted British officers with field glasses surveying the American positions, which they reported to Gates. Gates said in response, "Order out Morgan to begin the game."

Other than Morgan's riflemen, however, Gates was still reluctant to commit a larger force despite knowing full well that by this point his forces had a clear numerical superiority over Burgoyne's. This was the last straw for Arnold, who protested that the force was clearly insufficient and pressed Gates to send a larger force. Gates had finally had enough of Arnold, yelling at him, "You have no business here," Gates dismissed Arnold, but he also sent a brigade led by Brigadier General Enoch Poor to support Morgan's assault on the British left, while Brigadier General Ebenezer Learned held the center of the left facing Burgoyne's German troops.

The two forces made contact in what came to be known as the Battle of Bemis Heights. Walworth described the climactic encounter of the campaign: "As the great Hudson, when suddenly loosened from his winter chains of ice, rushes with resistless force over all obstructions, so from their restraining earthworks the impetuous Americans poured furiously upon their adversaries in the front, while Morgan, like a mountain torrent, swept down the height upon Fraser's heroic band. So terrible was the onslaught that in less than twenty minutes the

British were thrown into confusion. Fraser, in his brilliant uniform, on a splendid war horse, rode from side to side of the right wing, encouraging and rallying the bewildered troops, and protecting every point with his flexible five hundred. Burgoyne, seeing the right wing in danger of being surrounded, now ordered Fraser to form a second line to cover a retreat. In attempting this manoeuvre Fraser fell mortally wounded, and was carried from the field. The division under Poor, with the same impulsive vigor, dashed up the hill upon the artillery and grenadiers of the British left, and drove them from their guns. Ackland brought them back, and recaptured the guns, which again fell into the hands of the Americans, who rapidly turned them upon the enemy, and drove them flying from the field. Ackland was wounded in both legs. He was a large, heavy man, but an officer took him on his back, and ran some distance with him. The pursuit was close, and the officer, fearing he would be captured, dropped his friend, and hurried on. Ackland now called out to the flying men that he would give fifty guineas to any man who would carry him into camp. A tall grenadier took him on his shoulders, but had not proceeded many steps when he and his helpless burden were taken prisoners."

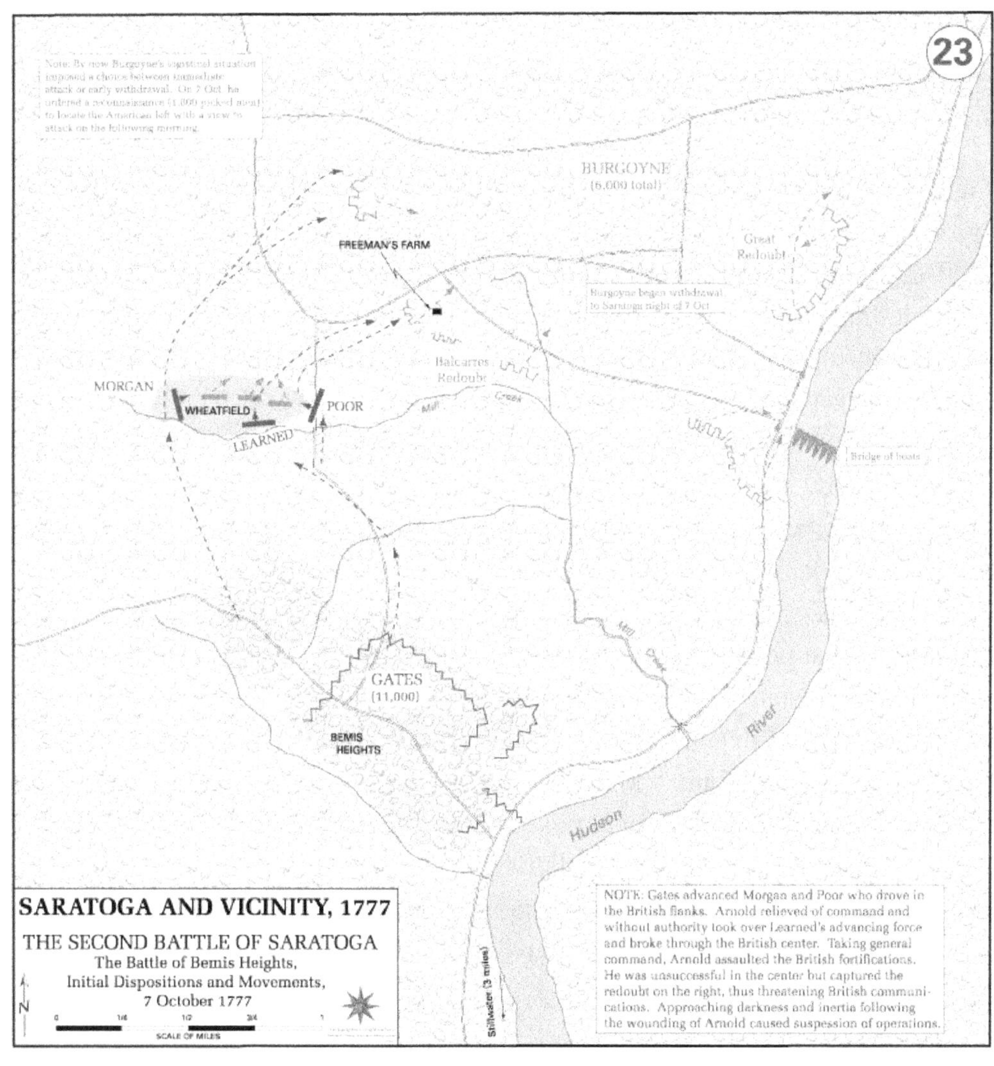

SARATOGA AND VICINITY, 1777

THE SECOND BATTLE OF SARATOGA
The Battle of Bemis Heights,
Initial Dispositions and Movements,
7 October 1777

N

0   1/4   1/2   3/4   1
SCALE OF MILES

NOTE: Gates advanced Morgan and Poor who drove in the British flanks. Arnold relieved of command and without authority took over Learned's advancing force and broke through the British center. Taking general command, Arnold assaulted the British fortifications. He was unsuccessful in the center but captured the redoubt on the right, thus threatening British communications. Approaching darkness and inertia following the wounding of Arnold caused suspension of operations.

A map of the positions ahead of the fighting

While Morgan and Poor were succeeding in turning the British right, the Germans held their ground in the center of the American's left. Into the battle rode Benedict Arnold who, some say in a drunken fury, rallied Learned's forces and drove at the Germans' positions. Walworth described the scene: "At this moment Arnold...excited into frenzy by the clash and roar of the battle, dashed like a meteor on the field, followed in the distance by Armstrong, Gates' aid-de-camp, carrying orders to compel his return. Stop the bison on his native plain? the swallow on its flight? More easy this than Armstrong's task. The genius of war thrilled Arnold's soul, as epic metres stir the poet, as rugged landscapes, shadowed under sunset lights, influence the artist's brain. Genius ever lives and conquers! It may be desecrated and destroyed, as Arnold buried his in ignominy; but while it lives and inspires its own peculiar work it rules and is supreme. Men bow before it, or lie crushed beneath its power. Thus, when Arnold waved his sword, and shouted his brief commands, the genius within him rung through the tones of his voice, glanced from the quivering flash of his sabre, and the regiments followed where he led — one strong will, one palpitating force. With two brigades he rushed upon the Hessian centre, who stood the shock bravely for a time, but as he dashed upon them again and again with a fury they had never witnessed, they turned and fled in dismay."

When General Fraser was mortally wounded, Burgoyne took command of the British forces personally, seeking to rally his shattered forces and stem the American advance. Walworth explained, "Burgoyne...was seen in the thickest of the melee, under the heaviest fire. Several shots tore his clothing, and his aids implored him not to expose himself, but resolute and daring, he endeavored skillfully, but vainly, to rally his army, and hold his ground. He could more easily have checked a hurricane on the great prairies; his whole force was driven before the storm, and swept into their entrenched camp. Here they made a determined stand…Arnold now took Patterson's brigade, and assailed Fraser's camp, where Balcarras and his light infantry had taken refuge. Charging with renewed vigor again and again up the embankment, he led the way over a strong abattis; driven back from this, he attacked the entrenchments connecting this redoubt with Breyman's flank defence. Here he succeeded, and leaving the Massachusetts regiments to follow up the advantage at that point, he encountered a part of Learned's brigade, and dashed upon the strong works of the Hessian camp. Here, too, he drove everything before him. Capturing the cannon, the artillerists fled in consternation, and Breyman was killed on the spot. Arnold's horse was shot under him; it fell on him, and his leg was severely wounded. He was carried from the field. The whole British camp now lay exposed to the pursuing Americans. Night and silence fell upon the scene. The groans of the wounded, the muffled words of command given for the burial of the dead, and the dirge-like wailing of the autumn wind in the tall pines, were the only sounds that followed the roar of artillery and the shouts of the victors."

A depiction of Arnold during the fighting

By the time night fell and the fighting ended, Burgoyne's plan for crushing the American rebellion, so carefully laid out for King George III in London just a few months before, lay in ruins on a wilderness battlefield in upper New York. Bemis Heights had cost him nearly 900 men killed, wounded, and captured, while American casualties are estimated at around 150. Among the British dead was General Fraser, who lived a few more hours. Returned to the British camp and informed by the surgeon that he only had a short time to live, Fraser is said to have cried, "O, fatal ambition! Poor General Burgoyne; My poor wife!"

Burgoyne moved his men from the field to their positions on the river bank, and on October 8, heavy skirmishing occurred as the British retrieved and buried their dead. At 9:00 that evening, Burgoyne ordered his army to retreat, leaving the baggage and wounded behind. Later, however, in a driving rainstorm at Dovagat, he ordered his men to halt. Walworth noted, "The imperious commander, who had led the forward march with unflinching resolution, pushing to his end without fear or hesitation, when foiled and sent back, for a moment shuddered, and refused to accept his fate. He still held his panic-stricken army under his will, and he determined once more to wait for the coming of the army from below; it might yet bring him relief."

Over the next two days, Burgoyne marched his tired and beleaguered army to Saratoga, arriving there on October 11. Gates followed Burgoyne, reaching Saratoga shortly after and encamping on the south side of the Fishkill River. Morgan's troops were posted on the heights near Saratoga Lake, in the rear and flank of the British camp. Burgoyne's forces were surrounded.

Walworth wrote that the British now realized "their camp was exposed in every part to the fire of cannon or riflemen; no approach to the river was permitted, and there was much suffering for want of water. The sick, wounded and women were huddled together in a house where cannonballs tore through the walls, and rolled across the floor, often wounding the helpless men who lay within. Madame Riedesel, with her children, and the other ladies took refuge in a cellar, where hours of horror were endured with uncomplaining misery."

As Burgoyne found himself trapped, General Clinton was advancing up the Hudson towards Burgoyne's positions. After capturing Fort Montgomery and Fort Clinton, the British destroyed the obstructions the Americans had placed across the river to impede a British advance by water, and they burned some American vessels. American forces retreated from the area, leaving the way to Albany undefended, but at this point, Clinton retreated after burning Kingston, leaving Burgoyne to fend for himself.

With only a few days of rations remaining, Burgoyne called his officers together on October 13. Walworth described the council of war: "'General Burgoyne solemnly declared, that no one but himself should answer for the situation in which the army found itself.' Three questions were then submitted for their consideration. '1st. Whether military history furnished any example of an army having capitulated under similar circumstances. 2d. Whether the capitulation of an army placed in such a situation would be disgraceful. 3d. Whether the army was actually in such a situation as to be obliged to capitulate.' These were answered in the affirmative, and there was an unanimous declaration in favor of capitulation. The terms of surrender were then discussed. A messenger was sent to Gen. Gates, who agreed to an immediate armistice. A meeting of officers to represent the commanders of the respective armies, was arranged to take place on the spot where Gen. Schuyler's house had stood."

Burgoyne proposed that after the surrender, his army should be marched to Boston and from there shipped to England. Gates refused, demanding an unconditional surrender and the British be held as prisoners of war in the colonies. Burgoyne rejected this, the armistice ceased, and the British prepared for the worst.

At this point, however, both Gates and Burgoyne received word of Clinton's assault up the Hudson. His fears aroused, Gates sent a message to Burgoyne agreeing to the British general's terms. Burgoyne agreed, and American and British officers set about negotiating some of the minor details of the surrender. When Burgoyne learned of Clinton's advance, he hurriedly called his officers together and asked if they could honorably withdraw their surrender and await Clinton's forces. To a man, Burgoyne's officers advised that such a move would be dishonorable. Thus, on October 17, Burgoyne and Gates agreed to the terms of a British surrender.

Walworth described the scene of Burgoyne's surrender, which represented the worst defeat suffered by the British up to that point in their history: "The British army were now marched out of their camps, under their own officers, to a plain near old Fort Hardy, where the Fish kill empties into the Hudson. Here, in the presence of only one American, an aid- de-camp of Gates, they laid down their arms. Generals Burgoyne, Riedesel and Phillips now passed over the Fish kill to the head-quarters of Gates, who rode out to meet them, accompanied by his aids. When they met, Burgoyne said, 'The fortunes of war, General, have made me your prisoner,' to which Gates replied, 'I shall ever be ready to bear testimony that it has not been through any fault of your excellency.' The American army were drawn up in ranks on either side of the road. The whole army of British prisoners, preceded by a guard bearing the stars and stripes, and a band playing Yankee Doodle, were marched between the files of their victors. Gates and Burgoyne stood contemplating the scene. In the presence of both armies, General Burgoyne stepped out, and drawing his sword from its scabbard, presented it to General Gates; he received it, and silently returned it to the vanquished General."

In the aftermath of the surrender, British forces withdrew from Ticonderoga and Crown Point in November, and they abandoned Lake Champlain by early December. The British troops who surrendered at Saratoga, the so-called "Convention Army," were supposed to be marched to Boston and shipped to Britain, with the stipulation that none of the men would take up arms in the Americas again. In order to make sure that this stipulation was enforced, Congress demanded a list of soldiers in the surrendered army. Burgoyne refused to provide such a list, so Congress decided not to honor the terms of the surrender. Instead, the British troops were kept in captivity as prisoners of war. While several officers were exchanged, much of the Convention Army as it was called was marched south to Virginia. The men were imprisoned there for several years, though many of them escaped and subsequently settled in the United States after the war.

As for Burgoyne, in the immediate wake of the surrender, he was a guest of Gates until he was exchanged for 1,000 American prisoners of war. After that, he returned to England, where he spent the next several years defending his actions before Parliament. In 1778, he was deprived of his rank, but it was restored to him in 1782 after a change of government. He was appointed a privy counsellor and named the commander-in-chief of forces in Ireland. He died on August 4, 1792.

The Aftermath of Saratoga

The importance of Saratoga would be clear in hindsight, but at the time, things remained quite tenuous for the rebels. Despite Washington's efforts, the defeat at the Battle of Brandywine on September 11, 1777 meant the path to Philadelphia lay open for the British. After retreating from Brandywine, Washington rallied and regrouped to make another attempt to stall the British advance on Philadelphia.

Washington's army continued to confront the British in Pennsylvania and New Jersey, but by late September, the British under Howe reached Germantown, Pennsylvania. Washington's army encamped in the Whitemarsh Valley, and Washington was determined to attack the British lines as soon as possible. After intelligence informed him that Howe had dispatched a considerable portion of his forces against American fortifications along the Delaware River, necessary for the British fleet to approach Philadelphia by water, Washington called a meeting of his general officers on September 28 to ask their opinion of an attack at Germantown. Anthony Wayne was one of a small group of officers who favored an immediate attack, while the other generals favored waiting until reinforcements arrived from the north.

The usually careful and prudent Washington took the advice of Wayne and the other generals who advocated an immediate attack. Thus, on October 3, Washington moved his 11,000-man army towards the enemy camp at Germantown. Wayne, with General Sullivan, comprised the right wing of the American forces, and Washington ordered them to march down Skippack Road towards the market-house in Germantown where the main body of the British forces were posted. Their advance was too rapid, and Wayne and Sullivan became trapped by the British forces when they were two miles ahead of the other American units.

The Battle of Germantown was the last major engagement of the year, and in the wake of their victory at Germantown, the British occupied Philadelphia, forcing the Continental Congress to flee from the rebel capital to nearby York. By then, however, news of the Battle of Saratoga was spreading across the states and heading for Europe.

Not surprisingly, the news of Burgoyne's surrender was a cause for jubilation across America. Congress adopted a resolution on November 1, 1777, declaring December 18, 1777 as a national day of thanksgiving and praise in recognition of the success at Saratoga. Washington issued orders for that day to be observed by the Continental Army, writing, "Being the day set apart by the Honorable Congress for public Thanksgiving and Praise; and duty calling us devoutly to express our grateful acknowledgements to God for the manifold blessings he has granted us, the General directs that the army remain in its present quarters, and that the Chaplains perform divine service with their several Corps and brigades. And earnestly exhorts, all officers and soldiers, whose absence is not indispensably necessary, to attend with reverence the solemnities of the day."

Ironically, this singular American victory, technically won by one of Washington's most frequent critics, did not immediately affect the material welfare of the Continental Army, as attested to by Private Joseph Martin's account of how the Continental Army celebrated that first national day of thanksgiving: "Well to add something extraordinary to our present stock of provisions – our country, ever mindful of its suffering army, opened her sympathizing heart so wide, upon this occasion as to give us something to make the world stare… a half gill of rice and a table spoon full of vinegar!" The next day, Washington marched his army into winter quarters at Valley Forge.

Benjamin Franklin had been sent by Congress to France in December 1776 to secure a critically needed alliance, and he was an ideal choice for Enlightened France, which revered

Franklin for his scientific accomplishments and his known reputation as a brilliant man. Franklin had also been a diplomat before the Revolution, spending several years in London on behalf of the colonies. However, the French refused to provide more than arms and money throughout 1777, until they learned in December 1777 about Saratoga and Burgoyne's surrender. With that news, French King Louis XVI entered into a formal military alliance with the United States, and in February 1778, France joined the war.

Meanwhile, as he looked for a place to establish his winter camp, Washington came across a small community known as Valley Forge. Located 20 miles northwest of Philadelphia, it seemed like an ideal location. There was plenty of empty land around the village in which his men could build shelters, and it was close enough to the British lines to keep an eye on their movements while being far enough away to keep them from attacking in force.

His army had repeatedly faced a lack of discipline and chronic disorganization, and Congress began to consider replacing Washington as commander after the fall of Philadelphia. General Gates, who had received the lion's share of the credit for Saratoga by marginalizing Benedict Arnold's role in the victory when he submitted his report to the Congress, was floated as an alternative, and Washington was understandably devastated. Making matters worse, the winter was unusually harsh, leading to an estimated 2,000 or so deaths in camp from diseases. Gouverneur Morris would later call the soldiers at Valley Forge a "skeleton of an army...in a naked, starving condition, out of health, out of spirits."

Despite the difficulties, it was at Valley Forge that Washington truly forged his army. He introduced a more rigorous training program for his troops, sponsored by Prussian General Friedrich Wilhelm von Steuben, who had fought with Frederick the Great. Like the Marquis de Lafayette before him, von Steuben came to Washington's army via the recommendation of Benjamin Franklin, who hoped to use their appointments to curry political favor internationally. Despite speaking little English, von Steuben went about drafting a drill manual in French, and he personally presided over training drills and military parades. With the help of von Steuben, the Continental Army left Valley Forge in the spring of 1778 a more disciplined army than ever before, and the worst of their failures were behind them.

France's entry into the war dramatically altered the strategic balance. The war became a global war, with much of Great Britain's possessions threatened. As a result, Great Britain was forced to spend more resources outside of the American theater. British strategy had to change to accommodate a global war; Great Britain had to protect its colonies in the West Indies, India and even guard against a potential French invasion of Ireland.

French participation also had an immediate effect on Great Britain's North American strategy. Prior to France's entry, Great Britain could move troops and supplies by sea with only minimal threat from American privateers. But France had a powerful navy that could threaten British troop movements, and attack British-held towns from the sea. Thus, the British would shift their strategy to trying to subdue the South.

During the Revolution, Gates nearly leveraged the victory at Saratoga into successfully undermining Washington's position at the head of the Continental Army, but today the battle is more closely associated with Benedict Arnold. American history books credit Arnold for the American success at Saratoga, and it cannot be understated how important Arnold's achievements were to the cause from 1775-1777, but given his subsequent treason, it would be shortsighted if not downright imprudent not to consider what his motivations were even in serving there. Perhaps George Washington provided a succinct perspective when he said Benedict Arnold's left leg, which had been so badly wounded at Quebec and Saratoga, "was the only patriotic part of his body." Washington said that if and when Arnold was captured, "his leg should be cut off and buried with full honors," while the rest should hang. Benjamin Franklin himself wrote, "Judas sold only one man, Arnold three millions." In the years following the Revolutionary War, it was discovered that Benedict Arnold wasn't the only American officer approached by the British to betray the cause. Several other disgruntled men were targeted, including John Sullivan, Daniel Morgan, Philip Schuyler, and Israel Putnam. However, they all rejected British overtures, which makes Arnold's decision appear that much more heinous.

At the close of 1777, it could honestly be said that Benedict Arnold had been the colonists' greatest war hero, with his string of successes being longer and more crucial than anyone else in the Army, including George Washington. It could even be argued that the Revolution may have been lost without his service at places like Ticonderoga, Lake Champlain and Saratoga. And on top of it all, Arnold had spent a small fortune of his personal money financing his own actions, during which he was badly wounded many times and literally became a cripple in service to his country.

After Saratoga, Arnold headed to the Continental Army at Valley Forge, where he was feted with applause and took one of the first U.S. Oaths of Allegiance. The following month, Washington placed Major General Arnold in command of Philadelphia, as French entry into the war had compelled the British to quit the rebel capital.

Unaccustomed to power, Arnold began entering into business arrangements and capitalistic ventures even before reaching Philadelphia. On top of that, Arnold demonstrated his taste for luxury and extravagance, and in short order there were plenty of local Philadelphians upset with him. How Arnold truly felt before he met the Loyalist Peggy Shippen in Philadelphia is unclear, but it wound up being the most important connection Arnold made in the city. Shippen was from a well-to-do Loyalist family, and while the British occupied the city the year before Peggy had made the acquaintance of John André, who was serving in General William Howe's command. André paid particular attention to Peggy. Peggy maintained contact with André even after the British left Philadelphia. After a brief courtship, Arnold married Peggy in April 1779, right around the time his court martial was being resolved. It's widely believed by historians that

Peggy helped induce Arnold's treason, and it was obviously her relationship with her "dear friend" John André, who had become General Henry Clinton's spy chief, that made Arnold's communications with the British possible.

Given what ensued at West Point, it became impossible for Americans to fully acknowledge Arnold's contributions to the success of the Revolution, and for that reason, America has taken on a unique way of commemorating Arnold's military career.

The most famous example can be found on the Bemis Heights battlefield. There, the inscription on the Boot Monument, which commemorates the spot where Arnold was injured during the battle, captures the manner in which the country has traditionally handled the process of acknowledging Arnold's extraordinarily important accomplishments for America while always keeping in mind the fact that he is the nation's most infamous traitor.

"Erected 1887 By

JOHN WATTS de PEYSTER

Brev: Maj: Gen: S.N.Y.

2nd V. Pres't Saratoga Mon't Ass't'n:

In memory of

the most brilliant soldier of the

Continental Army

who was desperately wounded

on this spot the sally port of

BORGOYNES GREAT WESTERN REDOUBT

7th October, 1777

winning for his countrymen

the decisive battle of the

American Revolution

and for himself the rank of

Major General"

The Boot Monument

Arnold received the same treatment in the Victory Monument at Saratoga, which also manages to acknowledge him without naming him. At that monument, the four greatest American heroes of the battle are commemorated with statues on one side of the monument. Gates, Schuyler, and Daniel Morgan all have statues, while one side remains empty, where Saratoga's greatest hero should have had a statue. Likewise, in John Trumbull's famous painting of Burgoyne's surrender, nearly two dozen rebel officers are depicted, but there is no sign of Arnold.

The Victory Monument

It would literally take centuries for modern historians to offer a more nuanced perspective of Arnold's career and Saratoga's place in it. Historian James L. Stokesbury may have put it best when summing up Arnold's story: "Ever since 1780, a host of writers from serious historians to respected novelists have attempted to rehabilitate Arnold, without any convincing success. [One point that needs to be made] is that if honor was more touchy then than now, so principles were more flexible. Private and public business were inextricably mixed; patriotism, nepotism, and graft were accepted ways of managing affairs; reasonably honest men might seek accommodation in a family quarrel, and accept rewards for doing so. In other words, the line delineating treason was not very clearly drawn. None of this obviates the fact that Arnold crossed it."

Arnold himself came to understand the ramifications of his decisions, including the action at Saratoga. In his final years, Arnold lived in England, where he would die on June 14, 1801 a miserable and broken man. A favorite American legend claimed that when Arnold was on his deathbed, he stated, "Let me die in this old uniform in which I fought my battles. May God forgive me for ever having put on another." The story is almost certainly apocryphal, but there is no question that Arnold ultimately lived to regret his decision, and he stated he wished the bullet at Bemis Heights had hit his chest, not his leg.

The Shift South

"If he (Cornwallis) joins Phillips, I shall tremble for every post except Charleston." – General Henry Clinton

The American Revolution had been underway for nearly six years when Lord Charles Cornwallis began his Virginia campaign in April 1781. When France joined the war in earnest, the British shifted their focus south, but the British effort to subdue the southern colonies began to fail. A series of battles with American forces began to weaken the British, even though the British repeatedly forced the Americans to retreat. After the Battle of King's Mountain in present day eastern Tennessee, various guerrilla units linked up with organized American armies led by Major General Nathaniel Greene and Brigadier General Daniel Morgan. Morgan and Greene pushed the British general northward into Virginia, where Cornwallis chose to encamp in the Yorktown peninsula in March of 1781.

The South had seen little action during the war, but the British thought the area was more loyal and would offer less resistance. Initially, it seemed the British plan might work. Though loyalist allies were few, the British did find useful friends in the Cherokee Indians. Together, the British and Cherokee were able to control the coastal regions of North and South Carolina and Georgia by the end of 1779.

The British thus began to fortify Yorktown on the York River. The York River was navigable for the British Navy, and the British hoped to be able to resupply the southern theater of war from Yorktown. Washington and his men had stayed in the northern colonies throughout that time, but he decided in 1781 to coordinate movements south with the French toward Virginia. Washington's American forces and allied French troops combined north of New York City and feinted movement toward it to freeze the British in place before turning the army south to Virginia.

Meanwhile, the French navy in the Western Hemisphere sailed to the Chesapeake Bay, blockading Yorktown. The French were able to maintain this blockade and defeated a British Navy effort to break it in the Battle of Chesapeake Bay.

This was the state of affairs facing British planners as they considered their options for 1781. What could be done to snuff out this rebellion once and for all? It was never going to be easy; and now they faced an additional challenge in the form of France.

France had been formally allied with the United States since 1778, but it was only in the summer of 1780 that significant French forces had reached the theater, in the form of a small fleet under Comte de Barras and about 6,000 troops commanded by the Comte de Rochambeau. Initially disembarked in Rhode Island, by the close of 1780 these units had seen little action, but 1781 would be an entirely different matter.

Rochambeau

The mere existence of Barras' fleet, which consisted of eight ships of the line plus support, served to challenge the dominance of the Royal Navy. And by July 1781, Admiral De Grasse had arrived in the French West Indies with a further 20 battleships and transports. They picked up the local garrison of 3,000 French troops and headed for American waters, but they still had to figure out where they would be landing.

The opening of the campaign season in 1781 indicated that the British would continue their southern strategy, now centered on the Carolinas. The previous year had seen generals Henry Clinton and Charles Cornwallis capture Charleston in May, after which overall commander Clinton had returned to New York and left Cornwallis in command in the south.

Clinton

Cornwallis

The relationship between these two men was one of the most important factors underlying Britain's conduct of the war during this period. Clinton tended to be optimistic, but strategically cautious. His subordinate Cornwallis found this attitude frustrating. Cornwallis was impetuous, and a good tactician who happened to be strategically naïve.

Clinton's glib assumption that South Carolina was now under effective British control was typical of his mindset. As so often in the past, American forces were quick to regroup and once again pose a threat to the British soldiers and the territory they held. In August 1780, Cornwallis' regulars had thrashed Horatio Gates' American army at Camden, but only two months later the Americans had wiped out a small British force at Kings Mountain. These small-scale engagements would tip the scales of war backwards and forwards repeatedly, but neither side was inflicting a decisive blow.

For the 1781 campaign, Gates was replaced by the highly competent Nathaniel Greene, who together with Daniel Morgan harried Cornwallis's troops in a game of cat and mouse through

North Carolina. This approach favored the Americans, given their ability to withdraw and regroup, while Cornwallis had to rely on only occasional reinforcements from New York. In January 1781, Morgan beat a force under Banastre Tarleton at Cowpens, and in March the campaign reached its crisis at the battle of Guildford Courthouse. Cornwallis attacked vigorously, ousting the Americans from their powerful position but at a considerable cost. At one point in the battle, Cornwallis took the desperate measure of ordering grape shot artillery to be fired into the close battle lines, fully aware that the artillery would hit some of his own men along with the Americans.

A portrait of Tarleton

Cornwallis' ruthless tactics eventually carried the day, but once again, the British had merely won a hollow tactical victory because they were in no position to capitalize on it. Short on supplies and with greatly depleted regiments, Cornwallis had failed in his efforts to subjugate the far south. His options narrowing fast, in April he turned north into Virginia.

In this move, so fundamental to the future of the conflict, Cornwallis did not consider himself to be shifting to the defensive. Instead, Cornwallis believed that a British offensive into the Virginian heartland would crush the rebellion in the south, an opinion supported by the British Secretary of State for the American Department, Lord Germain. Virginia was the most populous state outside of New England and mostly anti-British. Cornwallis could not have imagined that the arrival of the redcoats would be greeted any differently than had been the case further south, but as he wrote to Germain, he thought Virginia was the "seat of the war". Germain agreed.

From his headquarters in New York, Clinton took a slightly different view. He saw Virginia as a subsidiary sector, worthy of limited commitment based on raiding and harassment. To this end he had already deployed a couple of thousand troops under generals William Phillips and Benedict Arnold, who was already notorious among the patriots even before he burned Richmond. Washington had already instructed his subordinates to summarily hang Arnold if they captured him in the South.

Engraving of Phillips

Cornwallis planned to rendezvous with the other generals and drive inland, but Clinton wanted to use the navy to extract some of Cornwallis' troops north to New York, where he faced the bulk of the American army under Washington and now Rochambeau's 6,000 French troops. By now, Rochambeau had marched south from Rhode Island to join up with Washington, but political pressure from London ultimately stayed Clinton's hand. Cornwallis was left in Virginia with a series of ambiguous and often changing orders.

General Phillips had died by the time Cornwallis linked up his men with Phillips' army and Arnold's men in May. Cornwallis now assumed command of a joint force totaling about 7,000 troops and took the offensive. Arnold, meanwhile, was recalled to New York.

Cornwallis' opponent in Virginia was the Marquis de Lafayette, the French noble who had been serving with the American forces since 1777. Lafayette's much smaller army wisely avoided pitched battles, but nonetheless made its presence felt and successfully screened Philadelphia. In June, 2,000 Continental troops arrived as reinforcements for Lafayette, which evened things up considerably.

Lafayette

Meanwhile, Cornwallis was ordered to stick to the Virginia coast and to secure a base for the Royal Navy. There was again talk of sending some of his regiments north. Portsmouth was the obvious choice, and in July he headed back south across the James River in order to secure it.

In doing so, Cornwallis came close to trapping the shrewd Lafayette at the Battle of Green Spring on July 6, but local commander General "Mad Anthony" Wayne extricated the Americans before Cornwallis could complete his victory. And on the 21st, more orders came from Clinton to remain on the York peninsula, which required crossing the James River again. Portsmouth was an excellent mooring for battleships, but it was difficult to defend. Cornwallis had to select a new base for the Royal Navy, and he had to be mindful of the threat posed by the French fleet. The tiny port of Yorktown therefore entered his thinking for the first time.

With its deep anchorage, and its position on a narrow inlet to the York River, Yorktown seemed to fit the bill. Artillery could be placed on both sides of the strait, which at this point was only half a mile wide, making it easy to defend the port from naval assault. Cornwallis arrived at Yorktown on August 2, and most of his army arrived over the following week.

Initially, Cornwallis began a leisurely reconnaissance, thinking mainly about the naval dimension and not considering Lafayette's army as a serious threat. But now his own small army was sitting on a peninsula, with the sea on three sides and a hostile enemy on the fourth. If by some chance the Allies gained naval supremacy, and if a larger army could be brought against him by land, Cornwallis had essentially cornered his men.

Communication between different commanders during the 18th century was a difficult and time consuming business. Historians have often been harsh on Clinton and Cornwallis, who were separated by 350 miles of ocean, but their failures also demonstrate just how well Washington and the French pulled off their own strategic coordination. To a degree they were lucky, since there was plenty that could have gone wrong, but their moves in the summer of 1781 showed astute strategic insight and a solid and trusting alliance. The bumblings of the British commanders, as had also happened only four years before at Saratoga, stand in stark contrast.

The French admiral De Grasse was in command of a large fleet in the West Indies with 3,000 French troops on board. He had orders to support the Americans on the mainland as best he could, but he must return to the West Indies in October because the French expected a separate British attack around that time. The seemingly obvious destination for De Grasse was New York. Clinton was sitting there passively with the main British army and a fleet under Admiral Digby. Washington was only 20 miles north of New York City with his Franco-American army. De Grasse could have linked his men up with Washington, neutralize the smaller British fleet and thereby facilitate the defeat of Clinton and the recapture of New York.

De Grasse

However, De Grasse wisely favored the southern option. He knew that there were small British and American armies operating on the Chesapeake shoreline and calculated that his own modest force of infantry might tip the balance better there. It was also closer to the West Indies, making it a shorter naval crossing and thus a smaller chance of having to tangle with the Royal Navy. The shorter distance also held out the possibility of achieving surprise, and even if things went disastrously, De Grasse could return to the West Indies that much faster.

De Grasse set sail in early August and skillfully evaded the powerful British fleet in the Caribbean by taking an unconventional route north. Meanwhile, a message was sent to Washington, who learned of De Grasse's move on August 14.

Washington now made the decision that would win the war for the United States. Rightly discerning Clinton's timidity he left a small force under Heath at West Point and struck south with the bulk of the Franco-American army. Heath's job was to keep an eye on Clinton and to persuade him that his tiny force represented a serious threat to New York. Although Clinton would eventually attempt to relieve Cornwallis at Yorktown, Heath's activities would inject just enough uncertainty into the situation to add to his procrastination.

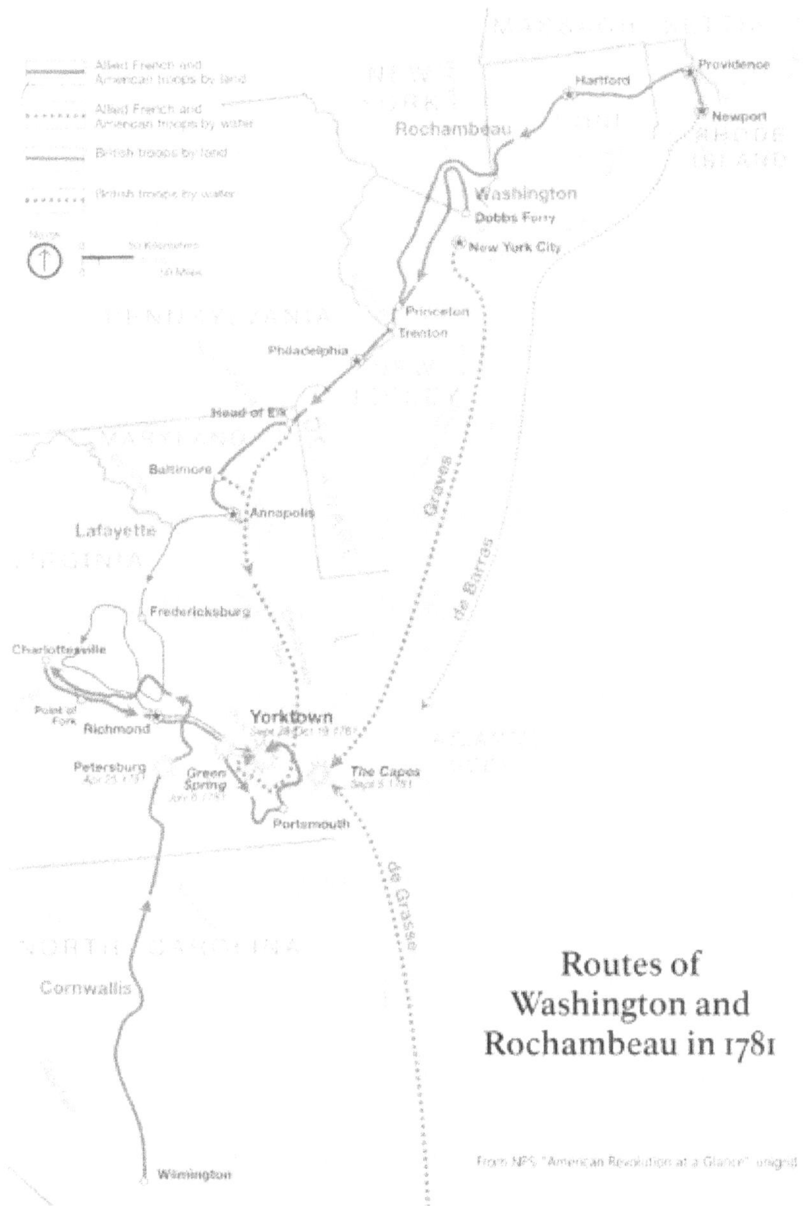

The routes to Yorktown

On land, Cornwallis leisurely prepared his defenses at Yorktown while Washington's force marched south to link up with Lafayette. Clinton stayed inactive in New York, watched by Heath's 2,000 men from West Point. Cornwallis had no clue that a far superior force was about to concentrate to his immediate west, blocking his land route from the York peninsula. And on the water, Cornwallis' emergency exit was about to slam shut.

When Cornwallis' scouts reported the sighting of French warships in the Chesapeake on August 30, he knew he had a serious problem. Over the next few days it became apparent that this was a large battle-fleet which included infantry transports, and that it might well be capable of sealing off Yorktown from the sea. That threat could only be countered by Britain's Royal Navy.

British Admiral Samuel Hood had been sent from the West Indies in pursuit of De Grasse with a force of 14 ships of the line. Taking a faster route, Hood had arrived at the Chesapeake before the French, found nothing, and thus kept moving north. At New York he joined Admiral Samuel Graves, bolstering the combined British fleet to a total of 19 ships of the line plus frigates and smaller vessels. The British were also concerned about Comte de Barras, who still had his squadron of eight battleships based on Rhode Island. In fact, Barras did plan to move south, escorting transports which would carry the bulk of Washington's heavy artillery to Virginia.

On August 31, Graves left New York in command of the combined fleet to sail south in search of Barras. At the time he did not know that De Grasse's force from the West Indies had since arrived in the Chesapeake and was busily disembarking troops. On September 5, the British fleet, with 19 ships of the line, encountered De Grasse and his 24 ships of the line. Initially, neither side knew how many ships the other had, leading the British to incorrectly mistake De Grasse's fleet for Barras. Ironically, De Grasse also thought it was Barras at first too. Only when more ships could be seen on the horizon did the two sides realize the extent of the enemy fleets, and De Grasse had so many ships that the British thought he had linked up with Barras.

By 9:30 in the morning, both sides were coming into their respective battle lines. The Battle of the Chesapeake was the culmination of a lackluster period in naval tactics, when opposing fleets would simply line up opposite each another to slug it out through attrition. Casualties were light and decisive actions were infrequent. Graves and De Grasse didn't know it yet, but their profession was on the cusp of a major evolution in tactics. Just six months later at the Battle of the Saints, the British would annihilate De Grasse's fleet in a close action melee, employing completely different tactics that would secure Britain's naval dominance for the following 150 years. Luckily for the Americans, the two hour skirmish between the British and the French in the Chesapeake was fought before that.

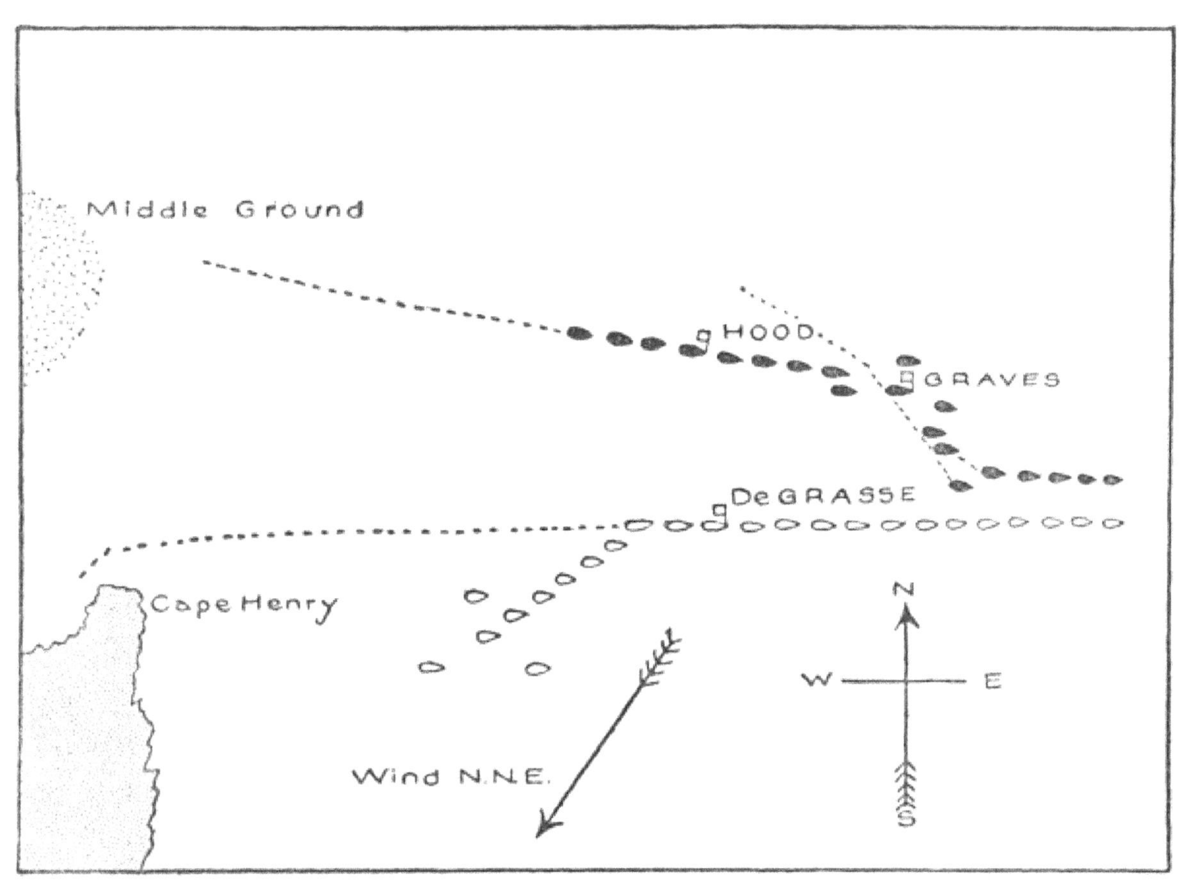

The battle lines

On September 5, the French had more ships, more guns, and the wind in their advantage, which allowed them to bring even more of their cannons to bear. In addition to a numbers advantage, the French also had bigger guns. The British and French fought for only a few hours during the afternoon, inflicting few casualties but badly damaging some of the ships on each side. The British would ultimately have to scuttle one of them as well. More importantly, the tactical draw was a strategic catastrophe for the British. Noting that "the French had not the appearance of near so much damage as we had sustained", Admiral Graves was compelled not to fight another battle against the French. This left De Grasse in control of the Chesapeake during an absolutely critical period of the war, and on top of that Barras' fleet arrived a few days earlier too. Graves took his own fleet back to New York, moaning about "the truly lamentable state we have brought ourself."

Cornwallis now found himself in a serious predicament. With the withdrawal of Graves' fleet and a large French presence just off the coast, any thought of naval evacuation was off the table. Meanwhile, enemy armies were marching to Yorktown. Cornwallis now realized he was facing the prospect of a siege.

Bottled Up

On September 14, Washington and Rochambeau arrived at the town of Williamsburg Virginia, twelve miles west of Yorktown. There they met Lafayette's holding force and discussed plans for besieging the British. Lafayette already had sound intelligence on the British works to date, which consisted of a double ring of defenses around Yorktown and fortifications across the York River at Gloucester Point.

Ebenezer Denny, a Major in the Continental Army, kept a diary of the campaign and discussed the arrival of Washington in Williamsburg:

> "Officers all pay their respects to the Commander-in-chief; go in a body; those who are not personally known, their names given by General Hand and General Wayne. He stands in the door, takes every man by the hand-the officers all pass in, receiving his salute and shake. This the first time l had seen the General. We have an elegant encampment close to town, behind William and Mary College. This building occupied as an hospital. Williamsburg a very handsome place, not so populous as Richmond, but situate on evenly, pretty ground; streets and lots spacious-does not appear to be a place of much business, rather the residence of gentlemen of fortune; formerly it was the seat of government and Dunmore's late residence. A neat public building, called the capitol, fronts the principal street; upon the first floor is a handsome marble statue of William Pitt.
>
> The presence of so many general officers, and the arrival of new corps, seem to give additional life to everything; discipline the order of the day. In all directions troops seen exercising and manoeuvring. Baron Steuben, our great military oracle. The guards attend the grand parade at an early hour, where the Baron is always found waiting with one or two aids on horseback. These men are exercised and put through various evolutions and military experiments for two hours-many officers and spectators present; excellent school, this. At length the duty of the parade comes on. The guards are told off; officers take their posts, wheel by platoons to the right; fine corps of music detailed for this duty, which strikes up; the whole march off, saluting the Baron and field officer of the day, as they pass. Pennsylvania brigade almost all old soldiers, and well disciplined when compared with those of Maryland and Virginia. But the troops from the eastward far superior to either."

Over the next few days, the bulk of the Allied army assembled at Williamsburg, many of them transported down the Chesapeake Bay in French vessels provided by De Grasse. In all, they had about 18,000 effectives. Of these, a small detachment had already been sent to join American militia facing the British position at Gloucester Point. The rest camped at Williamsburg while Washington made his plans.

By the 28th, all was ready. In accordance with a detailed set of orders, the Allies set off in two columns towards Yorktown. In the vanguard were riflemen and cavalry, ready to probe and disperse any British patrols that might be encountered. In case of more substantial opposition, the infantry regiments had field artillery interspersed between their columns. Washington would be ready should Cornwallis decide upon a field battle.

The heat was oppressive, even in late September. As the troops tramped through the close pinewoods, there were reports of several soldiers dropping dead of exhaustion and dehydration. For Washington, this may have been the riskiest day of the campaign; he could not afford to slacken the pace.

As the Allies approached Yorktown they split their columns to cover all three roads into the village. The French occupied the left side of the line, which brought them up to the northwest of the British position. The French forces reached all the way to the southern bank of the York River, to the west of Yorktown. The Americans had a slightly more circuitous route that took them to the south and southeast of Yorktown, with their right resting on the south bank of the river to the east of the British. Between them the two forces completed a semi-circular line, totally sealing off Cornwallis's position at Yorktown.

Positions at Yorktown

The French were the first to exit the woods and encounter British pickets. Shots were exchanged and light artillery pieces were used on both sides, with the British suffering some casualties. But by 4:00 p.m., the entire French force was coming into their designed positions and throwing up temporary earthworks in case of a British sortie. In most places they were about 300 yards from the British forces' outermost fortifications.

The American advance was impeded by the need to repair bridges destroyed earlier by the British, with the result that it was not until the 29th that the last of their field artillery came up to the line. Most of the heavier pieces were still en route, and it would not be possible to lay siege to Cornwallis in earnest until the big guns arrived and were put in position. Washington spent the entire day reconnoitering and studying the British positions.

The twin positions of Yorktown and Gloucester Point lay on the south and north banks of the York River respectively, where it opened out to the much broader Chesapeake Bay. The York

River was about half a mile wide at this point, meaning the British artillery was easily capable of providing a hot reception to any French man of war that tried to enter the river. The York River itself was patrolled by British frigates and sloops, effectively trapped by De Grasse's fleet, and Cornwallis also had dozens of small transport boats with which to communicate across the river. Thus, the French fleet lurked to the east, guarding the broad expanse of the Chesapeake from the Royal Navy, which had started to sail back to New York after the Battle of the Chesapeake less than a week earlier.

Gloucester Point was a hamlet garrisoned by a composite force of about 700 British troops, but it was an essential point for Cornwallis. It included a water battery capable of sweeping the York River entrance, it provided access to the Rappahannock peninsula and northern Virginia, which was full of rich farmland and ideal for foraging, and it served as a possible escape route for the entire army should the position at Yorktown become untenable.

On the south bank, Yorktown consisted of several hundred buildings, which were mostly wooden houses, warehouses and churches. It was a small, compact settlement with bluffs facing the river, which were ideal to deter an infantry attack, but it also presented a very dense target for enemy artillery, especially with an entire army attempting to crowd within its confines. Yorktown sat on the north shore of a narrow peninsula, delineated by the York River and the larger James River six miles to its south. In other words, Yorktown was already a geographic cul-de-sac, and the arrival of Washington's army had now restricted Cornwallis to Yorktown and its immediate defensive lines, together with Gloucester Point across the York River.

For a third of a mile in most directions, Cornwallis' troops had cleared the land of all timber to build defenses and create fields of fire. Rising terrain surrounded the village, which compelled the British to build an outer defensive work in order to deny that ground to the French and Americans. The cramped conditions inside the town itself also made a second line preferable. In some places near the French part of the line, the ground was cut through by marshy ravines, which made it difficult to concentrate attacking troops and easier to defend. The more open land lay to the south east, so that side of the British line had stronger works.

Cornwallis knew of his predicament, but he was still showing little sense of urgency. He first turned his attention to Gloucester Point, where a line of entrenchments and redoubts was constructed, incorporating several artillery batteries. It was only once that was complete that he ordered construction of the outer works at Yorktown. Making matters worse, Cornwallis had a small garrison and few good tools for digging. Although the pace of construction at Yorktown has been rightly criticized, his decision to concentrate on the outer works first was probably the right one. These could be used to delay the enemy while the inner works were completed.

18th century warfare wasn't very reliant on siege warfare, but the British defenses were thorough. The outer works consisted of a series of redoubts, strongpoints and batteries rather than a solid line. In all there were seven forts, with the star-shaped Fusiliers' Redoubt (built by the 23rd Regiment of Foot, the Royal Welch Fusiliers) on the extreme right of the British line. Moving down the left of the line, there was the Long Neck redoubt, followed by two smaller redoubts crowning "Pigeon Hill", a round hill in the center of the line. To the left of the rather weak Pigeon Hill forts was the Hampton Road battery, and on the extreme British left, two strong redoubts, known as numbers "9" and "10". There were other smaller works and trenches as well, and sources conflict on the precise nature of some of these positions, but modern archaeology has confirmed that Cornwallis' outer line was generally well constructed. It included abatis, which were felled trees that were used to delay advancing troops and break up their tightly packed lines, and the works also included ditches and palisades. Guns were taken from the Royal Navy frigates to supplement the light field pieces that Cornwallis had brought with him from North Carolina.

By September 20th, with the British fleet long gone, Cornwallis was in a position to commence building his inner line, while Washington's growing army was just 12 miles down the road. Although it was more continuous than the outer works, the inner line was put up in a hurry and was thus less robust in many places. There were eight redoubts connected by trenches and studded with artillery. Of these, the strongest was probably the "Hornwork", a large fortification in the center of the line. Behind the ramparts, earthen "traverses" radiated inwards, segmenting the defensive position. Their purpose was to mitigate enfilading fire, because the inner position was so small that shots from surrounding batteries would easily bounce laterally right through it, posing a grave threat.

The British had not neglected to defend the river either. In addition to the water batteries on both banks, at Yorktown they built palisades that ran right down to the water's edge, with the intention of preventing Allied troops from slipping along the narrow beach beneath the British guns. Finally, many of the smaller boats were deliberately sunk just offshore, creating a tangle of wreckage that would be difficult for an assaulting fleet to maneuver through.

Cornwallis' small army was a highly capable force. He had seven British line regiments, but these regiments were actually smaller battalions, and even those had seen their strength greatly reduced after months of campaigning. Nevertheless, one of the regiments included fierce highland troops, and there were also three elite Guards regiments. There were four regiments of German troops, which were on par with British line units, and two lesser units of Tory militia that had inadequate training. There was one small cavalry regiment, the 17th Light Dragoons, as well as the cavalry component of Tarleton's famous (or notorious) Legion of Loyalists.

Royal Navy gunners manned most of the heavier artillery, but it was no match for the weight of shot the Allies would eventually deploy. Although notional British strength at the beginning of the siege was about 7,500, modern historians estimate that sickness reduced this to about 5,500. That was still a lot of men to crowd into a village the size of Yorktown, and the shortage of space was exacerbated by the fact that many of the town's inhabitants had foolishly decided to stay. Also bottled up with Cornwallis was a large number of black slaves, ruthlessly exploited for labor and simply turned out of the British lines should they become sick. As usual, the overcrowded conditions led to the spread of illnesses, and even as the siege was just beginning, smallpox was becoming a problem.

When Washington's troops arrived on the 28th, Cornwallis' inner works were unfinished. Notwithstanding this, his outer fortifications were manned with several infantry regiments posted between and in advance of the main redoubts. Across the river at Gloucester Point, the 700 man outpost included plenty of field artillery. These troops were supposedly kept in check by a brigade of Virginia militia, but the Virginia militia had insufficient numbers or expertise to prevent the British from making a series of successful expeditions for food and supplies. As such, the siege at Gloucester Point was not truly worthy of being called a siege until early October.

Ebenezer Denny described the terrain in his front on the 28th:

"The whole army moved in three divisions toward the enemy, who were strongly posted at York, about twelve miles distant. Their pickets and light troops retire. We encamped about three miles off- change ground and take a position within one mile of York; rising ground (covered with tall handsome pines) called Pigeon Hill, separates us from a view of the town. Enemy keep possession of Pigeon Hill. York on a high, sandy plain, on a deep navigable river of same name. Americans on the right; French on the left, extending on both sides of the river; preparations for a siege. One-third of the army on fatigue every day, engaged in various duties, making gabions, fascines, saucissons, &c., and great exertions and labor in getting on the heavy artillery. Strong covering parties (whole regiments) moved from camp as soon as dark, and lay all night upon their arms between us and the enemy. Our regiment, when on this duty, were under cover, and secured from the shot by Pigeon Hill; now and then a heavy shot from the enemy's works reached our camp. Our patrols, and those of the British, met occasionally in the dark, sometimes a few shot were exchanged-would generally retire. Colonel Schamel, adjutant-general to the army, with two or three attendants, on a party of observation, ventured rather close; they were seen and intercepted by a few smart horsemen from the British. Schamel forced his way through, and got back to camp, but received a wound, of which he died next day. His death was lamented, and noticed by the Commander-in-chief in his orders. Possession taken of Pigeon Hill, and temporary work erected. Generals and engineers, in viewing and surveying the ground, are always fired upon and sometimes pursued. Escorts and covering parties stationed at convenient distances under cover of wood, rising ground, &c., afford support. This business reminds me of a play among the boys, called Prison-base.

At length, everything in readiness, a division of the army broke ground on the night of the 6th of October, and opened the first parallel about six hundred yards from the works of the enemy. Every exertion to annoy our men, who were necessarily obliged to be exposed about the works; however, the business went on, and on the 9th our cannon and mortars began to play. The scene viewed from the camp now was grand, particularly after dark-a number of shells from the works of both parties passing high in the air, and descending in a curve, each with a long train of fire, exhibited a brilliant spectacle. Troops in three divisions manned the lines alternately. We were two nights in camp and one in the lines; relieved about ten o'clock. Passed and repassed by a covert way leading to the parallel."

Dawn on Sunday, the 30th of September, brought a peculiar development to the siege at Yorktown. That morning, Allied patrols discovered that the British had abandoned most of their outer works. With the exceptions of the Fusiliers' redoubt on their far right, and redoubts 9 and 10 on their far left, the British had gone. They had pulled back to the now crowded and incomplete line hugging the cluster of houses by the riverside.

Washington and Rochambeau certainly wondered why the British moved back that morning, and for the most part historians are still trying to answer that question. It did seem strange that so much effort had been expended on the outer works, only to abandon most of them within 48 hours of the arrival of the enemy. Some have speculated that the British had hoped for a direct assault on the outer line. Thus, when it became clear that a conventional siege would ensue, they realized that they had too few troops to hold it. Others suggest that holding the outer line invited a flanking movement against the British left.

The likeliest explanation concerns the letter Cornwallis received from Clinton on the evening of the 29th. In it, Clinton promised to dispatch a large relief force consisting of 5,000 troops and 30 ships of the line under Admiral Digby. Clinton's letter said the relief force was scheduled to set sail on October 5. If he believed it, this could have motivated Cornwallis to shorten his line, operating under the belief that he would only have to hang on for another 10 days at most. Furthermore, Cornwallis could not have known just how powerful the array of American and French heavy artillery would be. Cornwallis' decision may have been made based on a combination of these factors.

The move, which was skillfully executed under the noses of the French and Americans, might have tempted them into launching an immediate assault on the town. This was part of the gamble that Cornwallis took, since it would have been costly and difficult to beat off such an attack while his troops were still sorting themselves out inside Yorktown. It didn't materialize, but the Allies did quickly move forward into the abandoned works. The French, anxious to secure the one remaining British position within their new line, attacked the Fusiliers' redoubt for several hours, but the British held onto the position despite three separate infantry assaults. They were aided by naval gunfire from their frigates in the river, an indication that Cornwallis had not stripped out all of the naval guns after all.

By the morning of October 3, both sides had reinforced their outposts over at Gloucester Point. The Virginia militia had been bolstered by the arrival of Continental soldiers, including Luazun's Legion, which also had light cavalry. It was time for the Allies to exert some control over the peninsula, rather than allowing the British free reign. In response, Cornwallis had sent Tarleton's Legion across by boat on the night of the 2nd. When Tarleton led his troopers out to escort a foraging expedition on the following morning, the stage was set for a sharp skirmish. The Allies had the better of it, and Tarleton himself narrowly avoided capture when he was unhorsed during a cavalry clash. The outcome was that the British retreated to their lines, having suffered 30-40 casualties, while the Americans were then able to invest Gloucester more closely. The free foraging represented by forays from Gloucester Point had been closed to Cornwallis; and any notions of an easy escape to the north had suffered a severe setback as well.

Meanwhile, Washington had been making preparations for a formal siege of Yorktown. Heavy siege artillery, including guns capable of firing 18 pound and 24 pound balls, had been arriving from the James River, where they had been shipped by French transport units. These monsters represented the heaviest ordnance of the campaign and were easily capable of smashing through the earthen and wooden defenses that Cornwallis had built. Cornwallis had nothing serious with which to reply, with less than a handful of 18 pounders; the vast majority of his guns were light field pieces. Between them, the Americans and French were able to assemble about 70 heavy siege guns and mortars at Yorktown; it was this firepower above all else that ended the siege so quickly. As both sides skirmished at Gloucester Point, Washington's big guns were lumbering towards the front.

The basic siege technique of the day was the construction of a series of "parallel" lines, from which the big guns could slowly encroach on the enemy's central position. From each parallel, the artillery would be used to batter the nearest redoubts and fortifications into submission, after which the sappers crept forward to build a new line. All the while, the besieging force would weigh up the possibility of a sudden assault, or indeed hope for a more peaceful resolution in the form of a parley or surrender. Those defending would hope for a relieving force, or that they could inflict sufficient damage on their attackers to trigger a withdrawal. Cornwallis' huge disparity in artillery made the last option entirely unrealistic, but he would not discover that until it was too late.

Of course, establishing a new parallel was a risky business, since the men digging the trenches were obviously vulnerable to enemy fire or counterattack. But Washington had a couple of important advantages to utilize. First, he had the numbers; with more than 18,000 effectives in a relatively short line, he had plenty of hands to rapidly dig trenches and regiments to spare with which to screen them. Conversely, Cornwallis hardly had the troops to scrape together a serious spoiling attack, and as it turned out the British would be surprised by the Allies' astonishing speed. Second, the nights were mild and cloudy, making it that much easier for the Allies to excavate right under the noses of the British. Perhaps most importantly, the soil was light and sandy, making it easier to dig extensive works in a hurry.

On the night of October 5, Washington's engineers crept forward and lay pine planking on the soft sand to delineate where they wanted the new trench to be dug. It was only about 800 yards from Cornwallis's inner defenses, easily within range for the big guns. The following evening, 2,500 French and American troops advanced beyond the line of pine planking. Their job was to screen the diggers by forming a silent, moonlit line of battle 20 yards in front of them in case the British attacked. No attack was forthcoming, and by the time the sun came up on the 7th, a shoulder height trench could be discerned ahead of the original Allied lines. Absent a successful British counterattack, for which Cornwallis really did not have the resources, all that remained was for the Allies to deepen and strengthen their new position and to bring up those guns. Washington and Rochambeau had plenty to be pleased about, but it was only when those guns opened fire that Cornwallis would truly understand his plight.

It took three days to develop the first parallel and install the first of the Allied siege artillery. By the time they had finished, they had some 73 heavy pieces in place. According to Henry Knox, Washington's artillery chief; that number was likely an approximation, with a precise number being difficult to determine due to the constant shifts of artillery during the siege. Either way, the artillery stretched right across the semi-circular British front, with good command of the river to the northwest near the Fusiliers' redoubt. This was in the French sector on the left of the Allied line, and they were ready a couple of hours before the Americans.

At about 3:00 p.m. on October 9, the guns in the French sector opened fire with a roar. The shot crashed into the British defenses, opening holes in the earthworks and knocking guns from their carriages. It was soon apparent that the Allied artillery far outclassed anything that Cornwallis could throw back, and attempts at counter-battery fire were short-lived. The British moved their guns away from their embrasures, hoping to save them for the final assault. In the river, HMS *Guadeloupe*, one of the troublesome frigates, was badly hit and started listing. The frigate pulled back across to the Gloucester side and was eventually scuttled. Two hours later, the firestorm was doubled, as George Washington himself set off the first of the American guns. One legend claims that the first shot hit a table where some British officers were eating, the kind of story that sounds too good to be true.

Depiction of Washington firing the first shot

Not the kind of general to leave the initiative to the enemy, Cornwallis attempted a deft outflanking maneuver the following day. Early on the 10th, he attempted to slip a battalion of infantry up the river and around the right flank of the American line at Gloucester Point. As Washington had feared all along, the northern enclave could be used by the British as a springboard for escape. Luckily for the French and Americans, expert French gunners on the south bank of the York River spotted the move and subjected the clumsy barges to a fierce bombardment. The planned amphibious assault broke up in disarray, and later that night the same battery fired heated shot at what remained of Cornwallis' river fleet. The 44 gun *Charon* was set ablaze, and several smaller boats took fire from her. By morning, the sloop *Formidable* was the only armed ship afloat. The siege could have been effectively won if the French navy had come up and taken control of the York River, but De Grasse was still anxious about the British fleet reappearing in the Chesapeake. He refused to move ships up the river.

Although the artillery bombardment of Yorktown could be observed from within the Allied lines, the French and Americans were unaware of the true chaos that they were inflicting. Playing it safe, Washington had ordered his artillery to keep firing even at night, which would make British attempts to repair the damage a hazardous occupation. Meanwhile, more accurate accounts came from the steady trickle of British and German deserters who fled across no man's land. In retrospect, it is quite likely that the barrage from the first parallel alone would have eventually been enough to force Cornwallis' surrender. On the morning of the 10th, he had received another letter from Clinton. Smuggled at night in an open boat right through the French fleet, the letter explained that maintenance issues had meant that the relief force would not now be leaving New York until the 12th at the earliest. This must have come as a bitter blow for the British commander, who until this point must have been expecting to see British sails on the horizon at any moment. His decision to pull back from the outer defensive line was now looking like a fatal mistake.

The World Turned Upside Down

It didn't take long for news of Clinton's letter to travel. By a twist of fate, and in a civilized gesture typical of the period, Cornwallis had allowed the elderly American patriot Thomas Nelson free passage to the Allied lines on the 10th. Nelson had heard of Clinton's letter and promptly notified Washington. For the Allies though, the thought of 30 British battleships and 5,000 fresh troops was a major worry, regardless of their timing. Pleased to learn of shaky British morale, Washington nonetheless knew he must quickly bring the siege to an end. The threat of Digby's British fleet or even the early departure of De Grasse for the West Indies could still lose the campaign. Furthermore, Cornwallis was an aggressive and dangerous opponent, so a desperate breakout attempt could not be ruled out either.

With all of that in mind, Washington made plans for a second parallel. On the night of the 11th, Allied troops again crept out of their lines to dig a new advanced position. This second parallel would be more confined than the first, because at both ends of this parallel the British still held dangerous outposts, including the Fusiliers' redoubt and redoubts 9 and 10. The new trench therefore ran across the center of the Allied position, stopping short of each flank. This new parallel was only 300-400 yards from the British inner works. Ebenezer Denny described the second parallel and the British redoubts in detail in his journal:

> "Second parallel thrown up within three hundred yards of the main works of the enemy; new batteries erected, and additional number of cannon brought forward- some twenty-four pounders and heavy mortars and howitzers. A tremendous fire now opened from all the new works, French and American. The heavy cannon directed against the embrasures and guns of the enemy. Their pieces were soon silenced, broke and dismantled. Shells from behind their works still kept up. Two redoubts advanced of their lines, and within rifle shot of our second parallel, much in the way. These forts or redoubts were well secured by a ditch and picket, sufficiently high parapet, and within were divisions made by rows of casks ranged upon end and filled with earth and sand. On tops of parapet were ranged bags filled with sand-a deep narrow ditch communicating with their main lines."

As on the first occasion, despite some minor skirmishing the new line was fashioned overnight and took the British completely by surprise. Once again the Allies immediately set about building batteries and redoubts into their new line so that they could move guns forward. All the while, the artillery from the first parallel continued to hammer at Yorktown and the fully exposed outposts. Nevertheless, the British redoubts, particularly numbers 9 and 10, also posed a serious problem for the Allies.

The Allies were nearly on top of the British at this point, so it could not be long before the casual slaughter of artillery fire at Yorktown gave way to the much more personal matter of infantry action. On the 13th, Washington concluded that it would be folly to continue work on the second parallel unless he could secure redoubts 9 and 10, which were positioned less than 200 yards away from the second parallel. Despite an incessant battering by Allied artillery, there was no sign of these two outposts falling or being abandoned. It would need to be done at the point of the bayonet. He convened a meeting of his staff and plans were drawn up for a simultaneous assault on both positions, to take place the following evening.

Illustration of Washington and Rochambeau giving orders before battle

At precisely 7:00 p.m. on the 14th, two infantry columns left the Allied lines close to the two redoubts. One was French and one was American. Each numbered about 400 men, all of them from elite units, including French grenadiers and light infantry and American light troops. Included in the assault were a large number of black troops from Rhode Island. The columns were led by sappers armed with axes; these men were to chop through the tangle of abatis which bedecked both British positions. In support were light artillery pieces, and Washington held two entire battalions in reserve. The attackers were to use stealth for as long as they could, with a silent approach and no gunfire until unavoidable. Washington went so far as to order the men to not reload their muskets until they were at the redoubt, by which point hand-to-hand fighting was likely to ensue anyway.

On the other side of the battlefield, yet another assault was launched at the Fusilier's redoubt, and across the river at Gloucester Point, French General Marquis de Choisy led an attack on the British line. These two moves are generally regarded as feints, and there is no doubt that Washington's main targets on the night of the 14th were redoubts 9 and 10, but these other attacks were made with vigor, and some historians have categorized them as serious assaults. But in both cases, they were beaten back with serious loss. For the fourth time, the troops in the Fusilier's redoubt had held off the French.

Things did not go as well for the British on their left. The American troops, led by Alexander Hamilton, targeted the smaller redoubt 10, which had only 50-70 defenders. Perched right on the cliff's edge by the river, this position represented the extreme left of the British line. 80 Americans crept around to its rear to cut off any retreat, while Hamilton and his main body clambered through the abatis. Along with cannon fire, sappers brought axes and hacked at the abatis to clear them as the soldiers moved forward. As the men charged, they climbed on each other's shoulders to get onto the parapet of the redoubt. The British offered fierce resistance, including the use of improvised hand grenades, and some Americans were hurt falling into craters in the redoubt left by their own artillery, but the sheer advantage in numbers eventually made the difference. Within 10 minutes, in what has gone down as one of the bravest assaults in American military history, Hamilton's men had captured the redoubt and its defenders, including the commander, Major Campbell. They had suffered only about 30 casualties. Sergeant William Brown became the first soldier awarded the Honorary Badge of Military Merit for his actions on the parapet, an award that would later be known as the Purple Heart.

Illustration of the assault on Redoubt 10

A few hundred yards to the left of the Americans, the French had a tougher nut to crack in redoubt 9. It was twice as large, with over 100 defenders, and the abatis proved difficult to remove. Many of the grenadiers were hit by musket fire as they waited for the sappers to cut a passage through, and the Hessians guarding the redoubt unleashed a volley on the charging French soldiers before engaging in hand-to-hand combat. It took the French 30 minutes to seize the position, losing at least 30 killed in the process. Some reports suggest that confusion in the darkness led to French soldiers inadvertently killing several of their own men. Ebenezer Denny described the fighting:

"On the night of the 14th, shortly after dark, these redoubts were taken by storm; the one on our right, by the Marquis, with part of his light infantry-the other, more to our left, but partly opposite the centre of the British lines, by the French. Our batteries had kept a constant fire upon the redoubts through the day. Belonged this evening to a command detailed for the purpose of supporting the Marquis. The night was dark and favorable. Our batteries had ceased-there appeared to be a dead calm; we followed the infantry and halted about half way-kept a few minutes in suspense, when we were ordered to advance. The business was over, not a gun was fired by the assailants; the bayonet only was used; ten or twelve of the infantry were killed. French had to contend with a post of more force-their loss was considerable. Colonel Hamilton led the Marquis' advance; the British sentries hailed them-no answer made. They also hailed the French, 'Who comes there?' were answered, 'French grenadiers.' Colonel Walter Stewart commanded the regiment of reserve which accompanied the Marquis; they were immediately employed in connecting, by a ditch and parapet, the two redoubts, and completing and connecting the same with our second parallel. The British were soon alarmed; some from each of the redoubts made their escape. The whole enemy were under arms-much firing round all their lines, but particularly toward our regiment, where the men were at work; the shot passed over. In about three quarters of an hour we were under cover. Easy digging; light sandy ground."

Illustration of the French attack on Redoubt 9

The murderous 30 minutes from 7:00-7:30 on the night of the 14th proved pivotal. Washington quickly rushed troops forward to secure the positions, and before daybreak, work had re-started on the second parallel, which could now be extended as far as the river, taking in the two redoubts as part of its line. On the following day, Cornwallis wrote: "my situation now becomes very critical". That was quite an understatement.

Over the next few days, the Allies worked hard to capitalize on the advantage they had gained by bringing heavy artillery forward to the second parallel. Sensing perhaps that this was the critical phase of the siege, and also mindful of the possible arrival of Digby's fleet, Washington and Rochambeau got the guns into action as soon as they could. Never completely finished, the Allies' second parallel was not as well fortified as its predecessor, but it wouldn't need to be because the British artillery had been mostly silenced by now. There had been a lively counter-barrage late on the 14th in response to the attack on the redoubts, but the British were now low on ammunition and exposing their guns risked immediate pinpoint bombardment from the French and Americans. As such, they tended to confine themselves to parabolic mortar fire and the occasional barrage at night. Ebenezer Deezy noted in his journal on the 15th, "Heavy fire from our batteries all day. A shell from one of the French mortars set fire to a British frigate; she burnt to the water's edge, and blew up - made the earth shake. Shot and shell raked the town in every direction. Bomb-proofs the only place of safety."

The American and French lines met in the center of their position, just to the left of the British Hornworks as looked at from Yorktown. At this point, there were two powerful batteries, one French and one American, with an infantry redoubt designed to protect them. Cornwallis had deduced that these were "breach batteries", specifically placed to knock a hole through the center of his earthworks ahead of a final infantry assault. That was exactly Washington's intention.

At 4:00 a.m. on October 16, 350 British troops crept forward to attack the breach batteries. They were elite soldiers, including grenadiers, guards and light infantry, just as Washington had used in his assault of the night before. This mission was unusual and exceedingly dangerous; they were being asked to spike the French and American artillery with a surprise night assault. Upon reaching the gun line they silently dispatched the French sentries with bayonets before fanning out left and right. The French battery on their right was taken completely by surprise, with the gunners asleep at their posts. In a few minutes, those who hadn't been bayoneted fled, and the British jammed bayonets into the touch holes of the guns and snapped them off in an attempt to spike the guns and disable them.

In the American battery there was more resistance, and some brutal hand-to-hand combat was fought. The attackers managed to spike three guns, but the French infantry launched a spirited counterattack that compelled a British withdrawal.

The British attack was as brave as it was desperate, but Cornwallis had squandered his surprise attack. His soldiers had not been properly equipped, and their crude attempts to disable the guns were repaired before noon. The attack was essentially made in vain.

A hint of autumn swept in across the Chesapeake that night. Rain lashed the bay and blew into a fierce storm. All day, the Allied batteries had smashed away at the British defenses, which were crumbling before their very eyes. Cornwallis had visited the Hornwork at the center of the barrage. His conclusion was that the British needed to breakout now or surrender. In the absence of Clinton's relief force, future resistance was a futile waste of life.

Cornwallis still had enough transports to ferry most of the army across to Gloucester in three or four trips, while leaving the wounded and a small rearguard behind at Yorktown. Once the brunt of the army was at Gloucester, Tarleton's guns would commence a brisk bombardment the following morning, and Cornwallis' entire command would attempt to punch through the Allied cordon and out into the Virginia countryside. This was something Washington had feared all along, and it was exactly why he had repeatedly urged De Grasse to station at least one of his big battleships in the York River. De Grasse had consistently refused to do that, insisting that he needed every gun to deal with Digby and pointing out that the ships would be at risk against British shore batteries.

As the storm lashed the Yorktown waterfront, the decisions made by both sides was about to be put to the test. Cornwallis' first regiments took to the boats comforted by the thought that the foul weather would obscure their move from the deadly French gunners behind the Fusiliers' redoubt. This proved to be the case, but the clumsy flat-bottomed boats were not fit for transport in such challenging conditions. Several foundered, and one drifted downstream to be captured by the Americans. Before midnight, the whole venture had to be abandoned, but by then some of the British soldiers had been transported to Gloucester. They would now have to be brought back across the river to Yorktown again. As the Allied bombardment picked up again early on the 17th, Cornwallis' damp troops were making their way back across the river.

Cornwallis was now out of good options. Later that morning, almost four years to the day after the British surrender at Saratoga, Cornwallis sent a white flag over to the Allied lines. When the French and American soldiers saw the white flag, they stopped firing and started cheering heartily. Washington himself ordered the men to stop cheering, shouting to them, "Let history huzzah for you." The officer carrying the white flag was blindfolded and brought behind the lines, touching off the beginning of two days of tense negotiations. The negotiations were carried on by two British officers, Lieutenant Colonel Thomas Dundas and Major Alexander Ross, Lieutenant Colonel Laurens for the Americans, and the Marquis de Noailles for the French. Washington ensured that the French side was treated as an equal belligerent, reflective not only of their vital importance at Yorktown but also to ensure no disputes could break down the terms between the French and Americans themselves.

It took two days of tense negotiation before the terms of surrender were finally signed on the morning of the 19th. Washington was determined to impose the same humiliating conditions on the British as they had meted out when Charleston had surrendered the previous year. Consequently, their banners were to be furled, meaning they would not enjoy the full honors of war. To 18th century soldiers, these things mattered. Far more important in concrete terms was the fact that the British soldiers would not be paroled. Except for the more senior officers, they were to remain in American captivity while hostilities persisted. In a concession to the British, and probably in an effort to get the deal done without further bloodshed, the troops at Gloucester Point were treated differently. Tarleton's cavalry would parade out of the British positions with their sabers drawn, in recognition that this bastion had not been forced to surrender.

That afternoon the American and French troops formed parallel lines alongside the Hampton road. The British regiments, by all accounts looking surprisingly smart after their ordeal, walked between these two lines to a field in which they stacked their arms. Legend has it that their musicians played "The World Turned Upside Down" as they marched, a nice story that is still often taught to schoolchildren but is almost certainly untrue. Cornwallis claimed illness on the 19th, leaving General O'Hara to offer the formal surrender. One woman who claimed to see the proceedings described O'Hara as "a large, portly man, full face, and the tears rolled down his cheeks as he passed along." As for Cornwallis, his absence was likely nothing more than a cowardly act from a man who owed better to his troops.

Even at the end, the British attempted a sly slight of the Americans. As O'Hara was formally presenting a sword to surrender, he presented it to Rochambeau. Fully aware of O'Hara's intent, Rochambeau refused and pointed O'Hara to present it to Washington. When O'Hara offered the sword to Washington, the general refused and made him present it to Benjamin Lincoln, the man who had attempted to surrender Charleston with full military honors the year before and received the poor treatment.

Ebenezer Denny jotted an entry on the 19th describing the surrender:

"Our division man the lines again. All is quiet. Articles of capitulation signed; detachments of French and Americans take possession of British forts. Major Hamilton commanded a battalion which took possession of a fort immediately opposite our right and on the bank of York river. I carried the standard of our regiment on this occasion. On entering the fort, Baron Steuben, who accompanied us, took the standard from me and planted it himself. The British army parade and march out with their colors furled; drums beat as if they did not care how. Grounded their arms and returned to town. Much confusion and riot among the British through the day; many of the soldiers were intoxicated; several attempts in course of the night to break open stores; an American sentinel killed by a British soldier with a bayonet; our patrols kept busy. Glad to be relieved from this disagreeable station. Negroes lie about, sick and dying, in every stage of the small pox. Never was in so filthy a place-some handsome houses, but prodigiously shattered. Vast heaps of shot and shells lying about in every quarter, which came from our works. The shells did not burst, as was expected. Returns of British soldiers, prisoners six thousand, and seamen about one thousand. Lord Cornwallis excused himself from marching out with the troops; they were conducted by General O'Hara. Our loss said to be about three hundred; that of the enemy said not more than five hundred and fifty. Fine

supply of stores and merchandise had; articles suitable for clothing were taken for
the use of the army. A portion furnished each officer to the amount of sixty dollars."

**One of the British flags surrendered at Yorktown. This flag is now on display in the
Smithsonian's American History Museum in Washington D.C.**

Across the water, a similar ceremony took place. Tarleton, famous for the barbarism of his ill-led Tory Legion, was rightly fearful for his life, but the Americans and French adhered to the terms of the deal to the letter, ensuring no atrocities. In fact, a little known provision of the surrender document allowed the British unfettered use of a French sloop to remove any persons or possessions they wished directly to New York. It seems likely that this was a face-saving means of smuggling out some of the Loyalists who may otherwise have been in danger. At Yorktown, Washington showed himself as good a diplomat as he was a soldier.

With that, the day was done. A second British army marched into captivity, and the American and French troops of Yorktown marched into history. The British relief fleet arrived in the Chesapeake five days later, managing to pick up a few stragglers who had escaped the siege, but by then about 8,000 British soldiers, over 200 guns, and all their muskets, transports and animals had surrendered.

When the American and French forces entered Yorktown, they were finally able to see some of the damage inflicted upon the place. Sarah Benjamin, a woman traveling with her husband in the Continental Army, described what she saw years later:

> "On going into town, she noticed two dead Negroes lying by the market house. She had the curiosity to go into a large building that stood nearby, and there she noticed the cupboards smashed to pieces and china dishes and other ware strewed around upon the floor, and among the rest a pewter cover to a hot basin that had a handle on it. She picked it up, supposing it to belong to the British, but the governor [Thomas Nelson] came in and claimed it as his, but said he would have the name of giving it away as it was the last one out of twelve that he could see, and accordingly presented it to deponent, and afterwards brought it home with her to Orange County and sold it for old pewter, which she has a hundred times regretted."

REDDITION DE L'ARMÉE DU LORD CORNWALLIS.

18th century French etching of the surrender at Yorktown

The surrender at Yorktown drove home the futility of British strategy in America. When he heard the news, Lord North, the British Prime Minister, remarked, "Oh God, it's all over." When news of Yorktown reached London near the end of 1781, popular support for the war plummeted. Before fighting resumed in 1782, Parliament had undergone a shift in power that stressed making peace. In April 1782, the House of Commons voted to end the war, ending the fighting in North America. However, the British would continue to fight the French in Europe and the West Indies until the Treaty of Paris was signed in 1783. The British also signed separate treaties with France and Spain at that time.

The most ironic aspect of the Treaty of Paris is that, despite helping turn the tide of the Revolution, and despite the fact the treaty was negotiated in its capital, the French ended up playing a relatively limited role in negotiating the treaty. Unbeknownst to the French, shortly after Yorktown, the British and Americans began conducting secret negotiations amongst themselves. While the Americans thought that John Adams would make a good negotiator to begin the long process of brokering peace with England, the French were not so sure. They insisted that the American government send other men whom they found more socially acceptable to join Adams. To that end, the tactful John Jay joined Benjamin Franklin and Adams in France, and together the three tried to open negotiations.

However, Jay and Adams soon realized that the French were not that keen on having America reunite with their perpetual enemy. It became apparent that whenever a French minister became involved in the process, negotiations slowed and even stalled entirely. So, against the advice of Franklin, the two men circumvented the French and began talking directly to the British commissioners.

Thus, the American delegation in France waited until the British and Americans had resolved much of their peace terms before informing the French. France was irate once it realized what the Americans had done, even with Franklin trying to soothe nerves and spin the events like a political operative, but by then it was too late for the French. Despite indebting itself to the tune of the modern day equivalent of hundreds of billions of dollars, France wielded almost no control over the terms of the peace.

The United States and Britain reached an impressively comprehensive peace in the Treaty of Paris. Among the important terms of the treaty, Britain recognized the colonies as free and relinquished territorial claims to them. The two sides then negotiated the boundaries that separated the United States from the British colonies in present-day Canada. Additionally, the British and Americans strove to share certain waters, including the Mississippi River and the fishing waters off Newfoundland. Finally, the two sides made mutual promises regarding paying debts and returning property that had been confiscated during the war, including slaves.

Still, the Treaty of Paris was not without its problems. Almost immediately, individual states in America rejected certain provisions and ignored them outright, a hallmark characteristic of American federalism that would lead to the Civil War 80 years later. Other problems included disputes along the boundary with Canada, and the fact that American access to the Mississippi River was blocked after the British and Spanish signed a separate treaty that left Spain in control of Florida. Some of these problems would fester heading into the 19th century, and eventually the British and Americans would go to war again in 1812.

The Treaty of Paris also had other geopolitical consequences. By ostensibly reconciling with the British, the Americans and French all but broke off their alliance, leaving Britain as America's natural trade partner. The choice between France and Britain divided the colonists: the Federalists viewed Britain as a more valuable trading partner, while Thomas Jefferson's camp identified with the French. The first political divisions between the men who would become Federalists and the men who would become Democratic-Republicans were already forming before the United States had even been recognized

As for the French and Americans, a similar partnership like the one between Rochambeau and Washington was not in the offing anytime soon. The United States and France would not be allies again until World War I, over 130 years after the siege of Yorktown.

It took two days for the two sides to work out the terms of surrender, and even at the end, one of the articles of the terms of surrender were not agreed to. Article X attempted to stipulate that any American colonist who had joined the British army would not be punished, thereby creating a blanket immunity for Loyalists. Washington didn't believe he could accept it, citing that it was a civil issue that a military commander could not adjudicate. It is also likely that Washington found that term repugnant and simply didn't want to accept it, an opinion harbored by many Americans. It was later noted, "The outcry against the Tenth Article was vociferous and immediate, as Americans on both sides of the Atlantic proclaimed their sense of betrayal."

> "Settled between his Excellency General Washington, Commander-in-Chief of the combined Forces of America and France; his Excellency the Count de Rochambeau, Lieutenant-General of the Armies of the King of France, Great Cross of the royal and military Order of St. Louis, commanding the auxiliary Troops of his Most Christian Majesty in America; and his Excellency the Count de Grasse, Lieutenant-General of the Naval Armies of his Most Christian Majesty, Commander of the Order of St. Louis, Commander-in-Chief of the Naval Army of France in the Chesapeake, on the one Part; and the Right Honorable Earl Cornwallis, Lieutenant-General of his Britannic Majesty's Forces, commanding the Garrisons of York and Gloucester; and Thomas Symonds, Esquire, commanding his Britannic Majesty's Naval Forces in York River in Virginia, on the other Part.

ARTICLE I. The garrisons of York and Gloucester including the officers and seamen of his Britannic Majesty's ships, as well as other mariners, to surrender themselves prisoners of war to the combined forces of America and France. The land troops to remain prisoners to the United States, the navy to the naval army of his Most Christian Majesty.

Granted.

Article II. The artillery, arms, accoutrements, military chest, and public stores of every denomination, shall be delivered unimpaired to the heads of departments appointed to receive them.

Granted.

Article III. At twelve o'clock this day the two redoubts on the left flank of York to be delivered, the one to a detachment of American infantry, the other to a detachment of French grenadiers.

Granted.

The garrison of York will march out to a place to be appointed in front of the posts, at two o'clock precisely, with shouldered arms, colors cased, and drums beating a British or German march. They are then to ground their arms, and return to their encampments, where they will remain until they are despatched to the places of their destination. Two works on the Gloucester side will be delivered at one o'clock to a detachment of French and American troops appointed to possess them. The garrison will march out at three o'clock in the afternoon; the cavalry with their swords drawn, trumpets sounding, and the infantry in the manner prescribed for the garrison of York. They are likewise to return to their encampments until they can be finally marched off.

Article IV. Officers are to retain their side-arms. Both officers and soldiers to keep their private property of every kind; and no part of their baggage or papers to be at any time subject to search or inspection. The baggage and papers of officers and soldiers taken during the siege to be likewise preserved for them.

Granted.

It is understood that any property obviously belonging to the inhabitants of these States, in the possession of the garrison, shall be subject to be reclaimed.

Article V. The soldiers to be kept in Virginia, Maryland, or Pennsylvania, and as much by regiments as possible, and supplied with the same rations of provisions as are allowed to soldiers in the service of America. A field-officer from each nation, to wit, British, Anspach, and Hessian, and other officers on parole, in the proportion of one to fifty men to be allowed to reside near their respective regiments, to visit them frequently, and be witnesses of their treatment; and that their officers may receive and deliver clothing and other necessaries for them, for which passports are to be granted when applied for.

Granted.

Article VI. The general, staff, and other officers not employed as mentioned in the above articles, and who choose it, to be permitted to go on parole to Europe, to New York, or to any other American maritime posts at present in the possession of the British forces, at their own option; and proper vessels to be granted by the Count de Grasse to carry them under flags of truce to New York within ten days from this date, if possible, and they to reside in a district to be agreed upon hereafter, until they embark. The officers of the civil department of the army and navy to be included in this article. Passports to go by land to be granted to those to whom vessels cannot be furnished.

Granted.

Article VII. Officers to be allowed to keep soldiers as servants, according to the common practice of the service. Servants not soldiers are not to be considered as prisoners, and are to be allowed to attend their masters.

Granted.

Article VIII. The Bonetta sloop-of-war to be equipped, and navigated by its present captain and crew, and left entirely at the disposal of Lord Cornwallis from the hour that the capitulation is signed, to receive an aid-de-camp to carry despatches to Sir Henry Clinton; and such soldiers as he may think proper to send to New York, to be permitted to sail without examination. When his despatches are ready, his Lordship engages on his part, that the ship shall be delivered to the order of the Count de Grasse, if she escapes the dangers of the sea. That she shall not carry off any public stores. Any part of the crew that may be deficient on her return, and the soldiers passengers, to be accounted for on her delivery.

Article IX. The traders are to preserve their property, and to be allowed three months to dispose of or remove them; and those traders are not to be considered as prisoners of war.

The traders will be allowed to dispose of their effects, the allied army having the right of preemption. The traders to be considered as prisoners of war upon parole.

Article X. Natives or inhabitants of different parts of this country, at present in York or Gloucester, are not to be punished on account of having joined the British army.

This article cannot be assented to, being altogether of civil resort.

Article XI. Proper hospitals to be furnished for the sick and wounded. They are to be attended by their own surgeons on parole; and they are to be furnished with medicines and stores from the American hospitals.

The hospital stores now at York and Gloucester shall be delivered for the use of the British sick and wounded. Passports will be granted for procuring them further supplies from New York, as occasion may require; and proper hospitals will be furnished for the reception of the sick and wounded of the two garrisons.

Article XII. Wagons to be furnished to carry the baggage of the officers attending the soldiers, and to surgeons when travelling on account of the sick, attending the hospitals at public expense.

They are to be furnished if possible.

Article XIII. The shipping and boats in the two harbours, with all their stores, guns, tackling, and apparel, shall be delivered up in their present state to an officer of the navy appointed to take possession of them, previously unloading the private property, part of which had been on board for security during the seige.

Granted.

Article XIV. No article of capitulation to be infringed on pretence of reprisals; and if there be any doubtful expressions in it, they are to be interpreted according to the common meaning and acceptation of the words.

Granted.

Done at Yorktown, in Virginia, October 19th, 1781.

Cornwallis,

Thomas Symonds.

Done in the Trenches before Yorktown, in Virginia, October 19th, 1781.

George Washington,

Le Comte de Rochambeau,

Le Comte de Barras,

En mon nom & celui du

Comte de Grasse.

Online Resources

Other Revolutionary Era titles by Charles River Editors

Further Reading about Saratoga

Bennett, William J; Cribb, John (2008). The American Patriot's Almanac. Thomas Nelson Inc. ISBN 978-1-59555-267-9.

Historical Society of Pennsylvania (1896). The Pennsylvania magazine of history and biography, Volume 20. Historical Society of Pennsylvania. OCLC 1762062.

Corbett, Theodore. (2012) No Turning Point: The Saratoga Campaign in Perspective. Norman OK: University of Oklahoma Press.

Ketchum, Richard M (1997). Saratoga: Turning Point of America's Revolutionary War. New York: Henry Holt. ISBN 978-0-8050-6123-9. OCLC 41397623. (Paperback ISBN 0-8050-6123-1)

Luzader, John F. Saratoga: A Military History of the Decisive Campaign of the American Revolution. New York: Savas Beatie. ISBN 978-1-932714-44-9.

Morrissey, Brendan (2000). Saratoga 1777: Turning Point of a Revolution. Oxford: Osprey Publishing. ISBN 978-1-85532-862-4. OCLC 43419003.

Murphy, Jim (2007). The Real Benedict Arnold. Houghton Mifflin. ISBN 978-0-395-77609-4.

Nickerson, Hoffman (1967) [1928]. The Turning Point of the Revolution. Port Washington, NY: Kennikat. OCLC 549809.

Pancake, John (1985). This Destructive War. University of Alabama Press. ISBN 0-8173-0191-7.

Randall, Willard Sterne (1990). Benedict Arnold: Patriot and Traitor. William Morrow and Inc. ISBN 978-1-55710-034-4.

Sawicki, James A. (1981). Infantry Regiments of the US Army. Dumfries, VA: Wyvern Publications. ISBN 978-0-9602404-3-2.

"Saratoga National Historical Park". National Park Service. Archived from the original on 2009-05-30. Retrieved 2009-06-23.

"Saratoga National Historical Park – Tour Stop 7". National Park Service. Retrieved 2009-06-23.

Bird, Harrison (1963). "March To Saratoga General Burgoyne And The American Campaign 1777". New York Oxford University Press.

Creasy, Sir Edward (1908). The Fifteen Decisive Battles of the World.

Furneaux, Rupert (1971). The Battle of Saratoga. New York: Stein and Day.

Mintz, Max M (1990). The Generals of Saratoga: John Burgoyne and Horatio Gates. Yale University Press. ISBN 0-300-04778-9.

Patterson, Samuel White (1941). Horatio Gates: Defender of American Liberties. Columbia University Press.

Savas, Theodore P; Dameron, J. David (2005). A Guide to the Battles of the American Revolution. Savas Beatie. ISBN 1-932714-12-X.

Ward, Christopher (1952). War of the Revolution, 2 Volumes. MacMillan.

Further Reading about Yorktown

Alden, John R (1963) The American Revolution, 1775-1783

Allison, R. (2011) The American Revolution: A Concise History

Black, J. (2001) War for America: The Fight for Independence 1775-83

Davis, Burke (1979) The Campaign that won America

Draper, Theodore (1996) A Struggle for Power: The American Revolution

Greene, J. (2009) The Guns of Independence: The Siege of Yorktown 1781

Griffith, Samuel B. (1976) In Defence of the Public Liberty: Britain, America and the struggle for independence from 1760 to the surrender at Yorktown in 1781

Hibbert, Christopher (1990) Redcoats and Rebels – The War for America, 1770-1781

Kemper, Dale French Win at Sea – Key to Yorktown Article first appeared in The Herald, issue 68, December 2005/January 2006.

Mahan, A.T., (1913) Major Operations of the Navies in the American War of Independence

Marston, D. (2002) The American Revolution 1774-1783

Wallace, Willard M. (1951) Appeal to Arms: A military History of the American Revolution

Wright, E. (1983) The Fire of Liberty